THE GREAT BOOK OF BRITISH USELESS INFORMATION

D0302607

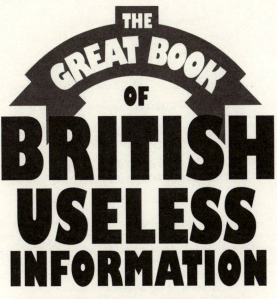

THE GREAT BOOK OF BRITISH USELESS INFORMATION

Everything you ever wanted to know about Britain

HANNAH WARNER

metro

Published by Metro Publishing
an imprint of John Blake Publishing Ltd
The Plaza,
535 Kings Road,
Chelsea Harbour
London, SW10 0SZ

www.johnblakebooks.com

www.facebook.com/Johnblakepub
twitter.com/johnblakepub

First published in hardback in 2009
This edition published in paperback in 2010

ISBN: 978-1-84358-253-3

All rights reserved. No part of this publication may be reproduced,
stored in a retrieval system, or transmitted in any form or by any means,
without the prior permission in writing of the publisher, nor be otherwise
circulated in any form of binding or cover other than that in which it is
published and without a similar condition including this condition being
imposed on the subsequent publisher.

British Library Cataloguing-in-Publication Data:

A catalogue record for this book is available from the British Library.

Design by www.envydesign.co.uk

Printed and bound in Great Britain by Clays Ltd, Elcograf S.p.A.

9 11 13 14 12 10

© Text copyright Hannah Warner 2009, 2010

The right of Hannah Warner to be identified as the author of this work
has been asserted by her in accordance with the Copyright, Designs and
Patents Act 1988.

MIX
Paper from
responsible sources
FSC® C018072

Every attempt has been made to contact the relevant copyright-holders,
but some were unobtainable. We would be grateful if the appropriate people
could contact us.

John Blake Publishing is an imprint of Bonnier Books UK
www.bonnierbooks.co.uk

CONTENTS

ACKNOWLEDGEMENTS

A massive thank-you to everyone who helped me put this book together, from press-office staff to librarians who efficiently responded to my every request. Thank you in particular to The Met Office © Crown Copyright (2007) for their assistance in the Weather section.

Thank you also to my brilliant family, without whom this book would never have been written. To my mum and dad, and Bill and June, who looked after the children on many occasions so I could get some work done. To Isabelle, Joe and Seth for being the best and most beautiful children in the world. And especially to Tim, for his constant support and encouragement (even though I'm sure he might have liked to have seen me at some point during the last six months and not have had to cook his own tea every night). I hope you enjoy it now it is finally finished!

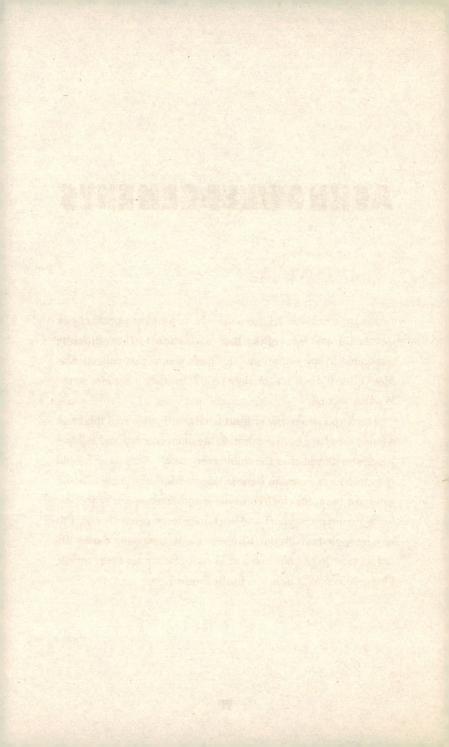

INTRODUCTION

I was talking to a French friend one day about British history, in particular the history of the British monarchy. Despite the fact that I am a history graduate, she was doing all the talking. She knew loads of stuff. I knew very little. It was very embarrassing.

She went on to talk about the places she had seen while walking along a stretch of British coastline. Yet again, she had learned more in just one decade of living here than I had learned in a lifetime. It was even more embarrassing.

I decided it was high time to improve my knowledge of our 'land of hope and glory'. This is what I discovered ...

GREAT BRITISH HISTORY

🐾 During the 1930s, women working for Directory Enquiries had to be at least 5 ft 3 in (1.6 m) tall, so they could reach the top of the switchboard.

🐾 When Westminster Abbey was first built, its congregation was less than sixty.

🐾 When Britain's first escalator was installed at department store Harrods in London in 1898, customers who travelled on it were offered brandy or smelling salts upon reaching the top.

🐾 Thirteen couples on board the ill-fated *Titanic* were on their honeymoon.

🐾 English sailors were given the nickname 'Limeys' because they used to drink lime juice to help prevent scurvy.

🐾 In 1945, the divorce rate was over three times higher than the pre-war figure.

At the height of the Great Plague in 1665, 7,000 people died every week.

Chastity belts were first devised during the Middle Ages to prevent married women from being unfaithful. They were usually fitted on women whose husbands were away fighting in the Crusades.

The highest number of registered births in a single year came in 1920, when an amazing 1,194,068 babies were born. Since 1972, there have not been more than 800,000 births in any given year.

At the end of the 18th century, Royal Navy sailors were so badly paid that many of them turned to theft to boost their income. They traditionally wore striped jumpers, which subsequently became synonymous with thieves.

It was mandatory to have a ponytail in the British Army until the early 19th century.

At one point during the 18th century, St Petersburg in Russia was sending 27 million quills a year to the UK.

Quills for right-handed writers came from the left wing of a goose, while pens for left-handers came from the right. Each bird supplied just ten to twelve good quills, and sometimes only two or three.

At the beginning of World War II, a Spitfire's machine-gun bullets would go straight through enemy aircraft without shooting them down, so they had to be replaced with exploding-shelled cannons.

At the end of the 1930s, Pinewood Studios in Buckinghamshire was producing more films than any other studio in the world.

On 1 May 1707, when the Act of Union between Scotland and England came into force, Scottish church bells played the tune 'Why am I so Sad on my Wedding Day?'

The first person ever to withdraw money from a cash machine was *On the Buses* star Reg Varney, who opened the world's first cash dispenser at the Enfield branch of Barclay's Bank on 27 June 1967. The maximum withdrawal at a time was £10.

Comedian Ernie Wise made the first call by mobile phone on 1 January 1985. From the middle of London's St Katharine Docks, he phoned mobile-phone operator Vodafone's headquarters at Newbury in Berkshire.

Guglielmo Marconi sent the world's first radio message on 11 May 1897, from Lavernock Point on the Glamorgan coast to Flat Holm island 3 miles (4.8 km) away.

Before prisons were built in the 12th century, those found guilty of committing a crime were mutilated so that innocent people could identify them as criminals.

Great Britain and America went to war in 1859 over a pig. The Pig War began on 15 June, when an American settler named Lyman Cutlar shot and killed a trespassing pig that belonged to Englishman Charles Griffin on the present-day San Juan Island in Washington state.

British naval hero Lord Horatio Nelson suffered from seasickness all his life.

The first call for film censorship in Britain came from the cheese industry in 1898, after Charles Urban released a scientific film, taken through a microscope, that revealed the bacterial activity in a piece of Stilton.

MP William Huskisson was the victim of the first fatal railway accident. He was hit by a train at the official opening of the Manchester to Liverpool line, on 15 September 1830.

The practice of putting a washable piece of fabric over the back of armchairs to keep them clean and prevent them becoming stained by greasy heads became popular in Victorian times, as a result of the rise in popularity of men's hair oil.

William Cavendish, the Fifth Duke of Portland, was such a recluse he built a network of underground rooms and passages under his home, Welbeck Abbey.

Surnames were not used in Britain until after the Norman Conquest of 1066. Prior to that time, people were known only by their first name.

In 1464, during the War of the Roses, Bamburgh Castle became the first in Britain to be shot at by cannons.

The first nursery school for young children whose parents had to go to work opened in Scotland in 1781.

The thistle was adopted as the emblem of Scotland during the 13th century. It is believed that during that period, an army of King Haakon of Norway, intent on conquering the Scots, landed at the Coast of Largs under cover of darkness. In order to move quietly and carefully, the soldiers removed their footwear. Unfortunately for the invaders, however, one stood on a thistle and shouted out in pain, alerting the Scots to the invasion. The attack failed.

When Britain abandoned the Julian calendar in favour of the Gregorian calendar in 1752, 3 September became 14 September and eleven days were 'lost'. There was a public outcry as people demanded the return of their eleven days.

Mary Queen of Scots wrote letters to her supporters in invisible ink while awaiting execution.

Venetia Burney from Oxford was just eleven years old when she came up with the name Pluto for the newly discovered planet, named after the Roman god of the underworld, in 1930.

The first air-mail letter was carried by balloon from England to France in 1785.

In 1385, the nuns of St Helens Bishopsgate in London, were reprimanded for their less-than-strict lifestyle. Among the things they were admonished for were 'the number of little dogs kept by the prioress, kissing secular persons, wearing ostentatious veils' and 'waving over the screen which separated the parish nave from the convent nave'.

The first pantomime to be performed in London was *The Tavern Bilkers*, which was staged at Drury Lane in 1702.

Lillian Lindsay became Britain's first female dentist in 1895.

During King Henry VIII's thirty-eight-year reign, he had more than 70,000 people executed. That works out as an average of just over five every day.

In 1939, on the eve of World War II, the Government designed three posters to steady the public's resolve and maintain morale. They featured the crown of King George VI set against a red background, and three slogans: 'Freedom is in Peril', 'Your Courage, Your Cheerfulness, Your Resolution Will Bring Us Victory' and 'Keep Calm and Carry On'. Two-and-a-half million copies of the latter were printed, to be distributed in the event of a national catastrophe – however, they were never used and remained in storage.

A total of 30,000 British soldiers were killed during the first thirty minutes of the Battle of the Somme. By the end of it, more than 1 million lives had been lost on both sides.

Explosions from the Battle of the Somme in 1916 could be heard on Hampstead Heath in London.

The first English woman legally to appear on the stage in England is believed to have been Margaret Hughes, who appeared as Desdemona in *Othello* at the Vere Street theatre in London on 8 December 1660.

The shortest war in history was between Great Britain and Zanzibar on 27 August 1896. Zanzibar surrendered in less than forty minutes.

There was no complete English translation of the Bible until the 14th century.

In 1631, two of London's most respected printers, Robert Barker and Martin Lucas, produced what they believed to be a faithful reproduction of the King James Bible. They made, however, one simple typographical error in the Book of Exodus, omitting the word 'not' from the seventh commandment 'Thou shalt not commit adultery'. Worried that people may regard this as permission to commit a sinful act the King, Charles I, demanded all copies of that version be destroyed, and fined the printers.

The nine of diamonds playing card is often referred to as the 'Curse of Scotland' because it was said to be the playing card used by Sir John Dalrymple, the Earl of Stair, to cryptically authorise the Glencoe Massacre of 1692.

During the Middle Ages, the job of an arming squire would be to tend to a knight's every need. This included cleaning the knight's armour after a hard day on the battlefield. On the outside there would be mud and blood, but the inside was far worse. Knights didn't get toilet breaks during battle.

Robins only became a symbol for Christmas in the 19th century, when postmen – who mostly brought mail at Christmas – wore scarlet waistcoats and were known as Robin Redbreasts.

Bank Holidays were introduced in 1871 by banker and MP Sir John Lubbock, who believed that it was important to encourage the working classes to play cricket. Until that time, the only holidays that the general working population had were Christmas Day and Good Friday, both of which were traditional days of rest and Christian worship.

The origins of the nursery rhyme 'Pussycat Pussycat' dates back to 16th-century England. One of Queen Elizabeth I's ladies-in-waiting had an old cat that roamed throughout Windsor Castle. On one particular occasion the cat ran beneath the throne where its tail brushed against the Queen's foot, startling her. Elizabeth decreed that the cat could wander about the throne room, on condition it kept it free of mice.

During the late 19th century, there was a craze for hats and bags made from hummingbird skins. One London dealer imported more than 400,000 in one year.

The first crossword in a British newspaper appeared in the *Daily Express* on 2 November 1924.

The first comic strip had appeared several years earlier: 'Teddy Tail' featured in the *Daily Mail* from 1915.

In 1264, Henry III pardoned Inetta de Balsham, who had been condemned to death for harbouring thieves. She had been hanged, but had survived after three days swinging on the end of the rope, as the result of a deformed windpipe. It was believed her survival was a sign from God that she was meant to live.

🐏 French mining engineer Albert Mathieu put forward the first-ever design for a Channel Tunnel in 1802, followed the next year by an English design proposal by Henri Mottray.

🐏 The first attempt at a tunnel excavation began in 1880, when the Beaumont & English tunnel-boring machine began digging undersea on both sides of the Channel. However, the process did not did begin in earnest until 1987.

🐏 One-third of the British population was illiterate when Queen Victoria ascended the throne.

🐏 Over 8 million horses died during World War I.

🐏 In order to be eligible for the state pension of five shillings a week when it was first introduced in 1909, you had to be over seventy, have earned less than £31.50 per year and to be of 'good character'. You were excluded if you were in receipt of poor relief, were a 'lunatic' in an asylum, had been in prison in the previous ten years, been convicted of drunkenness or were guilty of 'habitual failure to work'.

🐏 At the beginning of the 20th century, almost a quarter of the world's population lived under British rule.

🐏 During the late 1930s, Sir Robert McClean, chairman of Vickers, was looking for a name for the company's new fighter plane, one that sounded 'venomous' and began with an 's'. He rejected Shrike and Shrew before settling on Spitfire.

In 1917, all convicts were withdrawn from Dartmoor prison, which was regarded as one of the harshest prisons in the country, so it could be used to confine the 1,100 conscientious objectors who refused military service.

In 1305, King Edward I decided that the inch should be fixed at the length of three barleycorns.

The Royal Mail first allowed the sending of picture postcards in 1894. Thirty years later, 16 million were being sent every year.

The 1965 Toy of the Year was the James Bond Aston Martin die-cast car. It was followed in 1966 by Action Man, with the Spirograph taking the title in 1967, Sindy winning in 1968, and Hot Wheels Cars triumphing in 1969.

Researchers believe more British passengers than any other nationality died on the *Titanic* because they queued politely for lifeboats.

The last person to be beheaded in the UK was Simon Fraser, Lord Lovat, who was decapitated for treason at Tower Hill in London on 9 April 1747.

During World War II, one of Churchill's most important sources of information about what was really happening on the front line was the censored footage of the official newsreel, which was released in neutral countries. Censored footage included rolls of film from the Battle of Britain, which was regarded as too horrifying for the public to see.

England's first lottery began in 1567. It was created to fund the repair of harbours, fortifications and other public works under a royal proclamation issued by Elizabeth I. Tickets cost ten shillings each and the top prize was £5,000 – partly paid in cash and partly in plates, tapestries and good linen. Those who bought tickets were promised freedom from arrest of all crimes apart from murders, felonies, piracy and treason.

'God Save the Queen' was first performed in 1745 and is the oldest national anthem still in use today.

During World War II, the Red Cross sent more than 20 million food parcels from the UK to British prisoners of war. The parcels were carefully chosen to give the best dietetic value and to supply things that were lacking from prison camp diets. They contained: a 0.25-lb (113.4-g) packet of tea, a tin of cocoa powder, a bar of milk or plain chocolate, a tinned pudding, a tin of meat roll, a tin of processed cheese, a tin of condensed milk, a tin of dried eggs, a tin of sardines or herrings, a tin of preserve, a tin of margarine, a tin of sugar, a tin of vegetables, a tin of biscuits and a bar of soap.

Only 12% of homes in Britain had electricity in 1921.

BBC radio first broadcast the six-pip time signal on 5 February 1924, after setting up a joint venture with the Royal Observatory in Greenwich. The pips system was devised by the Ninth Astronomer Royal, Frank Dyson, in consultation with Frank Hope-Jones, the manufacturer of the free pendulum clock.

The cardigan was first worn by British soldiers to protect them from the cold during the Crimean War. It was introduced by James Thomas Brudenell, Seventh Earl of Cardigan. He is said to have paid £10,000 from his own pocket every year to make sure that his regiment was the most smartly dressed in the British Army.

In 1959, The Kew Gardens Hotel in London became the first British hotel or restaurant to install a microwave oven.

Until the end of the 14th century, fishmongers had their own court of law, known as the Leyhalmode, at which all disputes relating to fish were judged by wardens.

A total of 80% of middle-class households failed to adhere to the strict blackout regulations during the first few weeks of World War II.

During the Battle of Agincourt in 1415, in which King Henry V's English army of 6,000 defeated the French army of 25,000, the English archers fired up to twenty arrows a minute each.

The dungeon in the Tower of London was known as 'The Pit'. As it was below the high-water mark, the floor would become flooded during high tide and the chained prisoners would get their feet wet.

The first use of '999' for emergency telephone calls was in 1937. Originally the emergency number had been a single '1', but a change was made after too many accidental false alarms.

During World War II, Lord Louis Mountbatten led a project, codenamed Habbakuk, to build artificial icebergs that were to be used as aircraft carriers. Churchill abandoned the project however, when he realised that the carriers would cost over £6 million.

John Fletcher Dodd opened the country's first holiday camp in Caister-on-Sea, near Great Yarmouth, in 1906. The camp rules included a ban on alcohol, gambling, improper language and noise after 11pm. There were also fines for being untidy.

The Earl of Morton was beheaded by the guillotine, which he himself had introduced into Scotland.

Rudolph Hess, the deputy leader of Germany at the start of World War II, was the last person to be imprisoned in the Tower of London.

Britain's first nuclear submarine, which was commissioned in 1963, was HMS *Dreadnought*.

During the 17th century, burglars believed that they would never get caught as long as they carried a toad in their pocket.

The commercial Christmas card was invented in 1843 by Sir Henry Cole, the chief organiser of the Great Exhibition, pioneer of the Penny Post and founder of the Victoria & Albert Museum. Cole was said to have been bored with the idea of writing letters to people, so he hired an artist to create a pleasant scene for his festive correspondence instead. He soon worked out the financial potential of the item and put a thousand on sale.

Fireman Thomas Hart signed up to sail on the *Titanic* in 1912. He signed aboard at Southampton on 6 April with the rest of the engine stokers and firemen, but was listed as lost after the ship sank and his grieving mother began to make arrangements for her son's memorial service. She received a big shock, however on 8 May, when Hart walked into their Southampton home. It transpires he had got drunk after signing up for the voyage and had had his ship's papers stolen; they were then used by someone else to sign aboard. Following the theft, he had walked about Southampton in a confused state, too ashamed to return home. The identity of the person who had stolen Hart's papers, used them and was then lost has never been established.

In Tudor times, men believed that rubbing horse urine into their scalp would prevent baldness.

Executioners in Tudor times not only had to conduct the beheadings, but afterwards were responsible for boiling the heads and putting them on stakes.

The post-war British National Service Act was passed in 1947. National Service continued until 1963.

In England during the early 19th century, the average British worker would work up to ninety-six hours a week and earn just 40 pence.

In 1358, there were said to be only four public latrines in the whole of London, including one on London Bridge that discharged straight into the river.

🐾 The first public on-street convenience for men opened on 2 February 1852 at 95 Fleet Street, London, next to the Society of Art. Another, for ladies, opened on 11 February at 51 Bedford Street, Strand, London. There was a 2 pence entrance fee and extra charges for washing or clothes brushes. The new facilities were advertised in *The Times* and leaflets for them were also distributed; however, they had very few users and were eventually abandoned.

🐾 London's Pall Mall became the first street in the world to be lit by gas lights, on 28 January 1807.

🐾 The last recorded highwayman was George Cutterman, whose regular job was as landlord at the King's Head pub in Kirkington, North Yorkshire. He was responsible for dozens of robberies in the area, usually from travellers on the Great North Road. He was finally captured in 1824 and sent to York to go on trial. However, before reaching the city, he escaped by jumping from the top of the coach that was transporting him and was never seen again.

🐾 In 1942, the Church of England relaxed the rule that insisted all women had to wear hats in church.

🐾 In 1934, 1,476 tons (1,500 tonnes) of sand were spread on the shore at Tower Bridge to create an artificial beach for Londoners who couldn't afford a seaside holiday.

🐾 Only seven people were actually ever beheaded in the Tower of London itself. Most were taken outside to Tower Hill, where others could come and watch.

🐶 People sentenced to be beheaded were always advised to tip the executioner generously to help ensure that he would sharpen the blade of his axe and get the job done with just one blow.

🐶 The speaking clock was launched in the UK on 24 July 1936. It was the first of the pre-recorded phone information services, and was only available in the London directory area until it was rolled out nationally in 1942. In its first year it received almost 13 million calls. Today that figure is 135 million.

🐶 Jane Cane, a London telephone operator, was the original voice of the speaking clock from 1936 until 1963.

🐶 In the 19th century, people still received Christmas cards through the post on Christmas morning.

🐶 The origin of the phrase 'robbing Peter to pay Paul' came about when money that was raised by selling some land belonging to Westminster Abbey was used to repair the old St Paul's cathedral. Westminster Abbey is dedicated to St Peter.

🐶 Before English physician William Harvey proved that blood circulated around the body, doctors believed that blood was made in the liver and then turned into flesh.

🐶 British military authorities executed 312 British soldiers during World War I, mostly for desertion or cowardice.

When the British Army's Royal Flying Corps and the Royal Naval Air Service were amalgamated to form the Royal Air Force in 1918, it became the first air force to be independent of a nation's army or navy.

The first person to use an umbrella in Britain was London merchant, philanthropist and traveller Jonas Hanway. Upon returning to England from Persia in delicate health, Hanway could be seen around the streets of the capital using his parasol to keep the rain off his face and wig. He was often ridiculed for it, and for many years the umbrella was seen as something to be treated with scorn and suspicion. It was not until umbrellas were made out of attractive silk that they gained popularity.

Ultrasound became available to examine unborn babies in 1958.

The last known person to be eaten by a tiger in England was Hannah Twynnoy, a maid from the White Lion Inn, in Malmesbury. While visiting a travelling menagerie in the town in October 1703, she stood too near to the tiger's den, was seized by the tiger and was so badly mauled that she died.

The first British registered trademark was the red triangle of Bass & Co, which they put on their bottles of ale. It was registered on 1 January 1876.

Meanwhile, the first British patent was granted two-and-a-half centuries beforehand, when Rathburn & Burges were given Patent No.1 in 1617 for 'Engraving and Printing Maps, Plans &c'.

In 1314, while the Scottish army were fighting King Edward II, Scot James Douglas captured Roxburgh Castle after his soldiers disguised themselves as cattle. They used cow skins to get close to the castle before surprising its guards.

England's first public library was established in Winchester in 1850, in part of the former city jail.

Until the early part of the 19th century a tax was levied on all earthenware bottles and jars. By the 1830s, however, the total income the Government received from this was just £4,000 a year, not worth the expense of collecting it. Following the abolition of the tax in 1834, there was a huge rise in the sale of ginger beer, which was sold in stone bottles, and it became the most popular soft drink of the century.

The last invasion of Britain took place on 22 February 1797, when a French force of 1,400 troops landed near Fishguard in Pembrokeshire. However, the invasion is said to have soon lost momentum after the convicts discovered the locals' supply of wine.

The first name of Cambridge spy Kim Philby was originally Harold. He was born in India, where his father was working as a magistrate, and was nicknamed Kim after the hero of Kipling's novel, after he began speaking Punjabi before English.

Violinist John Banister organised the first-ever public concert for a paying audience in London in 1672. Formerly the leader of King Charles II's Court Band, Banister's concert was attended by forty-two people.

The Hundred Years' War actually lasted 116 years.

In 1757, British naval surgeon James Lind published a book recommending that sailors should receive rations of vitamin C-filled citrus fruit, as more sailors were dying from scurvy than in battle. It took an incredible forty years before the navy acted upon Lind's recommendation – yet as soon as they did, scurvy disappeared.

During the Middle Ages, more than 1,000 churches were built in Norfolk, of which more than 650 remain. It is still said to be the greatest concentration of churches in the world.

The Girl Guides' Association was formed in 1910, a year after a group of girl scouts turned up at the first public meeting of boy scouts at Crystal Palace.

During World War II, two pipelines were built between Britain and France to keep Allied forces supplied with fuel during D-Day. Codenamed PLUTO – PipeLines Under The Ocean – they pumped 172 million gallons (782 million litres) of fuel along 780 miles (1,255 km) of pipe at the rate of 1 million gallons (4.5 million litres) a day. 'Dumbo' ran from Dungeness to Ambleteuse near Boulogne, and 'Bambi' went from Hampshire through the Isle of Wight to Cherbourg.

English haberdasher John Hetherington was arrested for breaching the peace and fined £50 for causing a disturbance in London in 1797, when he wore his new creation, the top hat. Women fainted, men booed and a boy broke his arm in the crush that ensued as people rushed to get a look at the fancy headgear.

During the 18th century, the corpses of hanged men were often passed on to surgeons, who used them to show students how the body worked.

Following the execution of Sir Walter Raleigh in 1618, his widow had his head embalmed and carried it in a red leather bag, which she took wherever she went until her own death twenty-nine years later.

The world's first adhesive postage stamp – the Penny Black – came into use on 6 May 1840.

In the hot summer of 1858, the stench of sewage in the River Thames so offended MPs that Parliament was suspended and the Government agreed to take immediate action to deal with the problem. A leading Victorian engineer, Sir Joseph Bazalgette, was commissioned to design and build a system of sewers that would remove the sewage from the Thames, sending it instead to be treated in the East End at a new sewage treatment works in Beckton and Crossness. The sewers still form the backbone of London's sewage system today.

Ten-year-old King Richard II had to be carried out of Westminster Abbey following his coronation in 1377. He had collapsed under the weight of the heavy robes and crown.

During the Middle Ages, children would crawl under the scaffold where someone had been beheaded and scrape up any blood they could find for gory entertainment.

In the late 19th century, the Second Baron Rothschild owned a collection of exotic pets at his home in Buckinghamshire. Among them was a team of four zebras, which he used to pull his carriage.

Life expectancy in medieval Britain was between twenty and thirty years.

By 1851, life expectancy was still less than thirty years in industrial British towns.

The term 'Bedlam' derives originally from the Bethlem Royal Hospital in London, England, which was founded in 1247, and was the world's first psychiatric hospital. Not only did patients have to deal with horrendous living conditions, but they were also subjected to public scorn by those who were allowed to come in, for a fee, to watch, laugh at and aggravate them. Visitors were even allowed to bring in long sticks to poke inmates.

By 1600, 200,000 people were living in London.

During the 13th century, a polar bear was kept as part of the Tower of London menagerie. It would fish in the Thames for salmon while attached to a lead.

The first moving film – *Roundhay Garden Scene* – was shot in a Leeds back garden in 1880 by Louis Le Prince.

The Great Fire of London in 1666 cost the capital an estimated £10 million, at a time when the City's annual income was just £12,000.

More than 13,000 houses were destroyed during the Great Fire, with up to 200,000 people left destitute. Only five deaths were documented, however.

During the 19th century, some parents would lease their children to the local factory owners for as little as 12 pence a year.

The world's first chain store was WH Smith & Son, which began selling books and other goods at all stations belonging to the London & North Western Railway and the Midland Railway in 1848. They did not open any high-street stores until 1905.

MONEY, MONEY, MONEY

🐾 The Bank of England was set up in 1694 by William Paterson – a Scotsman. It was established to provide William III with finance to fight the French.

🐾 When the Bank was first set up, bank notes were hand-written, and although they were partially printed from 1725 onwards, cashiers still had to sign each note and make them payable to someone. The first fully printed notes were not issued until 1855.

🐾 The Bank of England produces £26,731,450 a day in banknotes. The Royal Mint is responsible for producing new coins, and issues 4.1 million per day.

🐾 William Churchill was the first person other than a monarch to appear on a British coin.

🐾 When the Bank of England was founded in 1694, the interest rate was set at 6%.

In 1989, a man bet £30 that by 2000 Cliff Richard would have been knighted, pop act U2 would still be a group and that *EastEnders*, *Neighbours* and *Home & Away* would still be on television. He was correct on all accounts and picked up £194,400.

A burnt loaf from the Great Fire of London sold for £322 at auction in London in 1996.

Guernsey islanders used French currency until the early 20th century. They used the French livre until 1834, with French francs being accepted until 1921.

The most expensive toy ever sold at auction was a Kammer and Reinhardt doll, which was bought at Sotheby's in London in February 1994 for £188,500.

A copy of the first issue of The *Dandy* from 1937, complete with free gift – a whistle – sold for £20,350 in 2004.

According to the Association of British Insurers, the number of dishonest motor claims detected has risen by 70% over the last three years, with figures showing that in 2008 insurers uncovered 24,000 fraudulent motor insurance claims worth £260 million.

A 2009 survey found the average weekly pocket money is now £6.32.

Britain's first income tax was introduced by Prime Minister William Pitt the Younger in January 1799 as a 'temporary measure' to help pay for weapons and equipment for the forthcoming Napoleonic Wars with France.

At its lowest, from 1874 to 1876, the rate of income tax was just 0.83%, while at its highest, between 1941 and 1946, the standard rate was 50%.

In the 19th century, counterfeiting cash became a capital offence, and dozens of people were hanged for it.

The UK's most valuable annual is *Beeton's Christmas Annual* from 1887, which features the first appearance of Sherlock Holmes and is worth over £75,000 today.

A 1965 letter written by John Lennon to his then wife Cynthia was sold for £17,250 in 1997.

Thirty-five minutes of film were taken off the director's cut of David Lean's 1962 epic film *Lawrence of Arabia*, so cinemas could fit in three showings of the film instead of two, and therefore take more money.

In March 2008, there were an estimated 26,922 million coins in circulation in Britain.

English traders are not legally obliged to accept Scottish banknotes.

When Prince Philip proposed to the then Princess Elizabeth, he was in the navy and earning just £9 a week.

In 1795, William Pitt the Younger introduced a tax on wig powder. If you powdered, you paid the equivalent of £30 a year in today's money. Tax records show it led to a marked decline in wig wearing.

In 1797, the British Clock Tax was introduced. The tax covered all timepieces, including watches and clocks. The annual tax rate was two shillings and sixpence for a basic watch, up to ten shillings for a gold watch. Clocks costing more than twenty shillings were rated at five shillings. People stopped buying watches.

In June 2006, a buyer paid £460,000 at auction for a rare medieval gold coin. The Edward III double florin, known as a double leopard, was circulated from December 1343 until July 1344 and had a face value of six shillings.

Before becoming world famous, the Spice Girls earned only £60 per week.

The metallic thread was introduced into banknotes in 1940, in an attempt to deter Nazi-inspired forgeries.

In January 2008, a 104-year-old British number plate bearing the registration 'F1' sold for £375,000. The previous record for a registration plate was 'M1', which sold for £331,000.

The current record for the highest auction price ever to be paid for a British artist was set in April 2006, when J.M.W. Turner's view of Venice called *Giudecca, La Donna della Salute and San Giorgio* sold for a massive £20.5 million.

The first British credit card was the Barclaycard, which was introduced in 1966.

Charles Dickens, Charles Darwin and Florence Nightingale have all appeared on the £10 note, while William Shakespeare, Michael Faraday, composer Edward Elgar and economist Adam Smith have all made it on to the £20 note.

Adam Smith was the first Scot to be featured on a British banknote.

A mystery bidder paid £115,000 for the nose cone from a Concorde at an auction of memorabilia from the supersonic aircraft, following its grounding in 2003. The new owner of the historic beak took it out of Britain and installed it in his house in Milan, Italy. In another lot, a Concorde toilet cubicle fetched £5,500.

Sir Terry Wogan earned £35 per programme when he joined the BBC in 1967 to present *Late Night Extra* on Radio 1 and Radio 2 every Wednesday evening.

Angela Kelly from East Kilbride in South Lanarkshire became Britain's biggest-ever lottery winner in August 2007 when she scooped £35.4 million in the EuroMillions draw. The draw took place on a Friday night, but she was not aware of her win until the following Monday. The lucky dip ticket was in her handbag and she only checked it when she realised the cash had gone unclaimed.

The first cheque known to have been drawn at a British bank was for £10, made payable to the bearer by Nicholas Vanacker. It was dated 22 April 1659 and was paid through Messrs Clayton and Morris, bankers, of Cornhill.

The earliest surviving printed cheque dates back to 4 March 1763. It was issued by Hoare's Bank, the first to introduce paper money and cheques to England, for £5,000 and was made payable to David Roberts by John Calcroft, Army Agent. Hoare's also issued the first cheques with perforated counterfoils on 5 July 1864.

The first cheque written out in British decimal currency was for £50.30. It was dated 4 March 1968 and was cleared by Westminster Bank, Crawley, Sussex, on 7 March.

Sir Sean Connery was paid £6,000 to star in the first James Bond film.

As soon as the *Titanic* went down in 1912, the ship's owners, White Star Line, stopped the wages of the crew.

Sir Tom Jones' first job was selling gloves, where he earned just £2 per week.

Former England captain Alan Shearer's £15 million transfer fee to Newcastle United meant that in 1996 he had to fly on a separate plane from the rest of his new team, as the travel insurance was too expensive.

In 2006, triathlon competitors were insured for £1 million should they have suffered injury by the Loch Ness monster. The cover was provided for more than a hundred athletes who were taking part in the Visit Scotland Adventure Triathlon.

🐶 Sales Director Graham Butterfield had his buttocks insured for £1 million after his employers, bed manufacturers Silentnight, realised that his rear was more sensitive than others when it came to testing out mattresses and made him their official 'bed bouncer'.

🐶 During World War II, the Germans set up Operation Bernhard, in which they attempted to counterfeit various denominations between £5 and £50, producing 500,000 notes each month in 1943. The original plan was to parachute the money into Britain in an attempt to destabilise the British economy, but it was found to be more useful to use the notes to pay German agents operating throughout Europe. Although the majority of notes ended up in Allied hands at the end of the war, forgeries frequently appeared for years afterwards, so all denominations of banknotes above £5 were subsequently removed from circulation.

🐶 The property market in Scotland was said to have reached an all-time high in June 2007 when a public toilet in St Andrews sold for almost £200,000.

🐶 In May 2008, BBC DJ Chris Evans paid £5.09 million for a Ferrari – making it the most expensive car ever sold at auction. The 250 GT SWB California Spyder was once owned by Hollywood actor James Coburn.

🐶 Britain only settled its World War II debts to the US and Canada when it paid two final instalments in 2005 andnd 2006. The payments of $83.25 million (£42.5 million) to the USA and $22.7 million (£11.6 million) to Canada were the last of fifty instalments since 1950 and nearly double the amount loaned in 1945 and 1946.

A lock of hair thought to have belonged to Jane Austen was sold at auction in Gloucestershire for £4,800 in June 2008. The auctioneers said the lock of hair was 'more of a gamble', as they could not prove if it was actually Jane Austen's.

A lock of hair belonging to fellow writer Charles Dickens also sold at auction in 2005. It went under the hammer for £3,120. This hair, however, was auctioned with a note of authentication from his sister-in-law and housekeeper Georgina Hogarth.

A dish containing a sample of penicillium mould, prepared by penicillin discoverer Alexander Fleming in 1935, sold for £14,950 at a 1997 auction at Christie's in London.

Employers in the UK can be insured against two or more staff leaving work permanently due to winning the National Lottery.

Rolling Stones guitarist Keith Richards has had the middle finger of his left hand insured for £1 million.

Insurers Lloyd's of London has taken out several unusual insurance policies for their clients, including insuring against death caused by disintegrating satellite pieces falling from the sky.

GREAT BRITISH FOOD AND DRINK

 More spam is sold in Egham than anywhere else in the country.

 People in southern England eat 6 million more cloves of garlic a year than those living in northern France.

 Bisto gravy granules got its name because it 'Browns, Seasons and Thickens in One'.

 The Kit Kat chocolate bar is said to have been named after the KitKat Club, an 18th-century Whig literacy club. As the building had very low ceilings, it could only fit in paintings that were wide but not too high. In the art world, such paintings became known as 'kitkats'.

 Carlsberg Special Brew was created specifically for Winston Churchill, as Denmark's thank-you for Britain's help during World War II.

The average price of a pint is 17 pence cheaper in the north-west of England than the south-east.

There are over 6,500 Indian restaurants in the UK.

Worcestershire sauce was created by John Lea and William Perrins in the 19th century at the request of Lady Mary Sandys, who on returning from India wanted a substitute for curry powder, which she was unable to buy in Britain at that time.

According to the Royal Society for the Prevention of Accidents, more than 14,000 Britons went to hospital in 2008 with compromising vegetable-related injuries.

Britain imports more Champagne than any other country.

The Aero bar was originally going to be called Airways to reflect the vogue for jet travel in the 1930s, when it was launched.

One of the earliest Mars Bars was pineapple-flavoured. It flopped.

Bovril was invented in 1886 by Scotsman John Lawson Johnston and was originally formulated to feed Napoleon's troops on the Russian front. Just two years later, over 3,000 bars and public houses were serving 'beef tea' in Britain.

Research by the British Heart Foundation in 2008 found that children's diets are now so poor that more than two-thirds of them do not think fast food is a treat.

On average, we eat 35 mince pies each over Christmas. As it takes 1 hour 27 minutes of walking to work off one mince pie, it would take 51 hours and 15 minutes to work off all 35.

The first Bakewell pudding, a jam pastry with a filling of egg and almond, is said to have been made by accident at the White Horse Inn in the Derbyshire market town of Bakewell in 1820. The landlady had asked for a jam tart, but her cook spread the eggs and almond paste mixture on top of the jam instead of stirring it into the pastry. The jam rose through the paste when cooked, but was so tasty that the mistake quickly became a popular dish among customers.

Despite having safe drinking water in this country, we spend £2 billion on bottled water every year.

British people are second only to the Swiss when it comes to chocolate consumption. The average Brit eats 20 lb (8.6 kg) a year – more than 6 lb 9.6 oz (3 kg) ahead of the Americans but still 3 lb 8 oz (1.6 kg) behind the Swiss.

The Lake District's most popular souvenir food is rum butter, which outsells the better-known brandy butter.

Unopened tins of Huntley and Palmer's biscuits were found in Scott of the Antarctic's hut on Ross Island, following his ill-fated final journey.

Paxo stuffing was invented in 1901 by John Crampton, a butcher from Eccles in Manchester, who wanted to make Sunday lunches more exciting. Business took some years to get going because stuffing is mainly served with poultry, which was a luxury at the time. When the price of chickens finally dropped in the 1950s and 1960s, Paxo's popularity took off.

Tea was rationed heavily during World War II. Each person was allowed only 2 oz (57 g) per week for twelve years from 1940. That would make just twenty cups of tea.

Tea was taxed heavily in the 1770s in Britain, which made it as desirable as alcohol for smugglers. The duty wasn't finally removed from tea until 1964.

The most expensive tea ever was sold in 1891: £36 15s was paid for 1 lb (0.5 kg) of Ceylon Golden Tips. That is the equivalent of £1,500 for 0.5 lb (250 g) today.

The average Briton drinks three cups of tea a day.

Kendal mint cake is said to have been first made during the 19th century, when a Kendal confectioner, intending to make glacier mints, took his eye off the cooking pan for a minute. On resuming his task, he noticed that the mixture had started to become grainy and cloudy, instead of clear. And when poured it out, the result was mint cake.

The world's largest-ever marrow was grown by Ken Dade in Norfolk in 2008, and weighed in at 143 lb (64.9 kg) — that's over 10 stone.

The first Indian restaurant in Britain was the Hindostanee Coffee House on Portman Square in London, which opened in 1773.

There are 362 registered vineyards in the UK, spread over 2,280 acres (923 hectares). In 2006, we produced 3.3 million bottles of wine.

The UK produces four times more white wine than red wine.

A 2009 survey by the Keep Britain Tidy group found that 29% of the litter from fast food found on Britain's streets was McDonald's wrappers.

Wine labelled as 'English wine' or 'Welsh wine' is made from grapes grown in England or Wales, whereas any wine labelled as 'British wine' is produced on the UK mainland from grape juice concentrate imported in bulk from abroad.

In 1674, the Women's Petition Against Coffee condemned the beverage 'as a little base, black, thick, nasty, bitter, stinking, nauseous puddle of water' upon which people should not waste their time or their money.

Over half of the espresso coffee consumed in the UK is drunk in the south-east of the country.

A total of 37% of coffee drinkers drink their coffee black, while 63% add a sweetener such as sugar.

Under European law, the word 'marmalade' can only be applied to fruit preserves made from citrus fruits. A product made with any other kind of fruit must be called 'jam'.

The world's biggest pancake was cooked in Rochdale in 1994. It was 49 ft (15 m) in diameter, weighed 2.95 tons (3 tonnes) and contained an estimated 2 million calories.

A 2008 study found that some 1.3 million unopened yoghurt pots are thrown away each day in the UK.

Before World War II, only half the British population had enough income to afford a healthy diet. Despite shortages, the health of Britons did improve during the war.

During the Middle Ages, butter was given an extra golden colour by being mixed with marigold flowers.

Chicken tikka masala is the dish most often ordered in Indian take-aways and restaurants in Britain.

The first chilled ready meal to hit the UK's shelves was chilli con carne. It was made in the late 1970s for Marks & Spencer.

The 1908 London Olympics were sponsored by Oxo, which was also given out to the marathon runners to help keep up their energy levels.

Cornish pasties were first made to be taken down the mines. The miners' wives would put their husband's initials in the crusts, so they could tell whose pasty belonged to whom.

A 2.1-oz (60-g) bar of ordinary milk chocolate contains seven teaspoons of sugar and approximately 0.6 oz (17g) of fat.

Although the Romans were known to enjoy a similar snack, the 'sandwich' did not become popular until the 1750s, when John Montagu, the gambling Fourth Earl of Sandwich, called for meat to be brought between two slices of bread, so he could continue gambling while he ate.

Badger meat was eaten in Britain up until World War II.

Only 20% of creatures caught by cats are birds. Most are mice and voles.

Jelly Babies were originally called Peace Babies when launched, to celebrate the end of World War I. Production stopped during World War II due to rationing, and it was only when it resumed in 1953 that the name was changed to Jelly Babies.

Bird's Custard was invented by Alfred Bird in 1837 because his wife was allergic to eggs, the traditional thickening agent for custard. Instead, Bird used cornflour mixed with milk to form his thick custardy sauce.

Biscuits date back to the 12th century. Richard the Lionheart is said to have taken 'biskits of muslin' to the Crusades.

In 2009, Cadbury, the makers of arguably Britain's most famous milk chocolate bar, decided to warn their customers that Dairy Milk contained – milk. In addition to listing milk in the ingredients, they said it was also necessary to print a warning saying 'Contains: Milk' in case people who were allergic to milk didn't realise that there was milk in Cadbury Dairy Milk.

Christopher Columbus is said to have brought chocolate back to Europe after he visited South America in about 1504; however, it only reached Britain in the 17th century. At that time it was made into a drink – but only for the wealthy, because of high import duties.

The first frozen food to go on sale in Britain was asparagus.

There are more Indian restaurants in London than there are in Mumbai or Delhi.

As the weather gets warmer there is an increase in sale of fizzy drinks in Britain. However, above 23 or 24 degrees Celsius (73.4–75.2 degrees Fahrenheit) people turn away from these drinks and instead look to bottled water to quench their thirst.

The first attempt to ensure that all food sold was pure and unadulterated came in 1860 with the Food Adulteration Act. Prior to this it had become commonplace to find the likes of leaves, twigs and gravel added to pepper; or grit, sand and ashes added to bread; while flour and arrowroot was sometimes added to cream to give it a thick appearance. Ten per cent of butter was also found to have had copper added to it in order to heighten its colour.

In 1864, the Privy Council estimated that one-fifth of butcher's meat sold in England and Wales came from diseased animals.

Peppercorns were once so expensive that the guards who unloaded them at the docks had their pockets sewn up to prevent them from stealing them.

The ring doughnut was invented by accident in 1847, by a baker's apprentice called Hanson Gregory, who pushed out the uncooked centre of the conventional doughnut that he had just pulled out of the deep fryer.

On average in the UK we eat 1,200 chickens each during our lifetime.

Quality Street chocolates were named after Peter Pan creator JM Barrie's once-popular play of the same name. They were advertised with the slogan 'Put your shop on Quality Street by putting Quality Street in your shop'.

Drambuie derives its name from an old Gaelic word meaning 'the drink that satisfies'.

During the Middle Ages, many Welsh people believed the leek had mystic virtues. It was claimed that girls who slept with a leek under their pillow on St David's Day would see their future husband in their dreams.

Rhubarb is often commonly believed to be a fruit, but it is actually a close relative of garden sorrel and is therefore a member of the vegetable family.

🐾 Cabbages were first grown in this country in Wimborne St Giles in Dorset, after a certain Sir Anthony Ashley brought them over from Holland in 1539.

🐾 The phrase 'cool as a cucumber' comes from the fact that the inside of a cucumber on the vine measures as much as 20 degrees cooler than the outside air on a warm day.

🐾 Marmite was first developed from leftover brewer's yeast in Burton-on-Trent in 1902.

🐾 Four out of five UK businesses believe the type of biscuit they serve to potential clients could clinch the deal or make it crumble.

🐾 A 2008 survey found the custard cream to be Britain's favourite biscuit, followed by the bourbon, the cookie and the ginger biscuit.

🐾 The average British adult will eat 35,000 biscuits during their lifetime.

🐾 Bananas (the world's most popular fruit) are bought by 95% of British households.

🐾 It is believed that strawberries were named in the 19th century by English children who picked the fruit, strung them on grass straws and sold them as 'Straws of berries'.

🐾 The first Starbuck's opened in 1998 in London on the King's Road in Chelsea.

The first McDonald's to open in Britain appeared in Woolwich in 1974.

The idea of picking your own produce originated in the 1950s with a handful of fruit farmers keen to supplement their income, which came principally from the regional wholesale markets. By the 1970s, there were 10,000 Pick Your Own farms.

Britain throws away about £20 billion worth of unused food every year – equal to five times our spending on international aid and enough to lift 150 million people out of starvation.

Blue Cheshire Cheese was once used to treat sores and wounds.

Mrs Beeton's first recipe for Victoria sponge cake didn't include any eggs.

Beeton was just twenty-nine when she died in 1865.

When Mrs Beeton died, her husband Samuel kept her death a secret from the public, fearing that the news would have an adverse affect on his wife's book sales.

Yorkshire puddings date back to the Middle Ages, when they were known as 'dripping puddings'. They were cooked underneath a spit of roasting meat, and served as the first course to the meal. In hard times, the puddings themselves replaced the meat as the main course. It wasn't until 1747 that the famous cook Hannah Glasse renamed them the 'Yorkshire pudding'.

Following World War II, sweets remained rationed until 1953.

Pimm's was invented in London in 1823 by James Pimm, a bartender in the City of London, to complement the oysters he served. It was originally sold as a health tonic – despite the alcohol content.

In 1688, William of Orange banned the import of foreign brandy to England, so some people began making imitation juniper brandy; it was known as gin.

Jack Cohen founded Tesco in 1919, when he began to sell surplus groceries from a stall in the East End of London. His first day's profit was £1 and sales £4.

The first own-brand product sold by Jack Cohen was Tesco Tea, which he launched in 1924. The name comes from the initials of TE Stockwell, who was a partner in the firm of tea suppliers, and CO from Jack's surname.

In 1617, King James I is said to have enjoyed a particularly tasty loin of beef at Hoghton Tower in Lancashire – so much so that he drew his sword and knighted the meat with the words 'Arise, Sir Loin', giving that cut of beef its name.

Typhoo tea was the first brand to be sold pre-packaged rather than loose over the counter. At the time, it was believed to have medicinal qualities and was sold through chemists' shops.

Pre-sliced, wrapped bread went on sale for the first time in Britain in 1930.

Sausages were introduced into Britain by the Romans.

The first-ever digestive biscuit was created in 1889 by a new young employee at McVitie's, called Alexander Grant. The name 'digestive' was derived from its high content of baking soda as an aid to food digestion.

The first company to sell ice cream from tricycles was Wall's in 1922. Their bikes were launched with the slogan 'Stop me and buy one'.

The first chocolate box was introduced by Richard Cadbury in 1868. He decorated a box with a painting of his young daughter holding a kitten in her arms.

During the 1930s, fish and chips became so popular that one shop in Bradford had to employ a doorman to control the queue at busy times.

During World War II, Lord Woolton, Minister of Food, declared that fish and chips was among the few foods not to be rationed as it was considered so important to the British diet.

Nearly a third of all chip-pan fire injuries occur between 10pm and 4am.

During the late Middle Ages in England, beer was used as a form of payment.

The average Briton eats an ounce (30 g) of cheese per person per day. Europeans eat almost twice as much cheese as we do, mainly because European breakfasts often feature cheese.

UK egg sizes are classified as: Small (53g, or 1.9 oz, and under); Medium (53–63g; 1.9–2.2 oz); Large (63–73g; 2.2–2.6 oz); and Very Large (73g and over).

In all, 10,775 million eggs are eaten in the UK every year, 8,643 million of which are produced in this country. Just 2% of these are sold by a butcher, while 2% are bought from a market stall, and only 1% are sold by a milkman. The vast majority – 85% – are sold through national supermarkets.

Around 700 varieties of cheese are made in Great Britain.

Although regarded as a traditional English drink, cider was originally introduced from France in the 12th century. Its name is derived from the Latin 'sicera', meaning 'strong drink'.

The first chocolate bar in Britain was sold by Fry & Sons in 1847, two years before John Cadbury brought his to market.

Jack's Bakery in Plymouth, which was established in 1597, is the oldest bakery in the world, and supplied biscuits to the Pilgrim Fathers, who left to colonise America in 1620.

In 1890, the makers of Smith's Patent Process Germ Flour decided the name of their product was too longwinded to use, so they decided to launch a national competition to find a new name, offering a prize of £25. The winner was Herbert Grime, who suggested 'Hovis', which was derived from the Latin 'Hominis Vis', meaning 'strength of man'. Hovis were so grateful to Grime for the name that when he died they paid his widow an annual pension.

Cans of carrots and veal supplied to the Royal Navy in 1824 were still edible when they were opened in 1936, some 112 years later.

The British eat potatoes about 10 billion times a year and pasta 1.4 billion times.

Four Pot Noodles are sold every second.

In 1903, Colman's of Norwich, the mustard makers, purchased a rival mustard manufacturer that was originally known as Keen & Son. The manufacturer had made their mustard a household name and spawned the well-known saying 'keen as mustard'.

The Penguin chocolate biscuit was one of the first biscuits to be advertised by name rather than by the company that manufactured it.

Crisps were introduced into Britain in 1913 by a grocer called Carter, who used a recipe he had brought back from France. They were not a success, however, until 1920, when Carter's manager Frank Smith set up Smith's Potato Crisps and began selling them throughout the country.

According to a 2009 survey, the most popular crisp flavour in Britain is cheese and onion, followed by ready salted, salt and vinegar, beef, prawn cocktail, chicken and bacon.

Cheese and onion, ready salted, and salt and vinegar crisps account for nearly two-thirds of packets of crisps sold in the UK.

In this country alone, we eat at least a tonne of crisps every three minutes.

In 1999, the Gloucestershire Hospitals NHS Trust changed the name of the traditional suet pudding 'Spotted Dick' to 'Spotted Richard', because it was thought patients might feel uncomfortable asking for the dessert. It was changed back in 2002 after it was decided patients were in fact capable of overcoming their blushes long enough to ask for it.

In old England, ale was drunk in pints and quarts. When customers got unruly, the innkeeper would tell them to mind their own pints and quarts and settle down, hence the expression 'mind your p's and q's'.

Heinz Baked Beans were first sold in Britain in London's upmarket department store Fortnum & Mason, where they were regarded as a luxury import.

The British eat twice as many baked beans per head as the Americans do.

One in six people in Britain goes to a fish and chip shop at least once a week.

A study by NHS Greater Glasgow found 22% of Scottish take-aways had deep-fried Mars Bars on its menu and another 17% used to sell them. Children were found to be the main buyers, with one shop selling up to 200 a week.

The first Bramley apple tree grew from pips planted by a young girl, Mary Ann Brailsford, in her garden in Southwell, Nottinghamshire in 1809. The tree is still standing and continues to bear fruit to this day.

Bassett's liquorice sweets were always sold separately, until the day in 1899 when company salesman Charlie Thompson accidentally dropped his bags of sweets, mixing them all up. The wholesaler he was visiting in Leicester expressed a keen interest in the mixture, and Liquorice Allsorts were born.

From the late 16th century, geese and turkeys were walked a hundred miles (160 km) from Norfolk to Leadenhall market in London each year. The mammoth journey would take three months and the birds wore special leather boots to protect their feet.

It takes 2.2 gallons (10 litres) of milk to make 2.2 lb (1 kg) of Cheddar cheese.

Cheddar is Great Britain's favourite cheese, accounting for 55% of the market – that's an incredible 295,262 tons (300,000 tonnes). Our second favourite is Mozzarella, the majority of which is made in this country.

🐑 Cheddar cheese was discovered more than 800 years ago, after a milkmaid let a pail of milk go bad while it was being stored in a cave at Cheddar.

🐑 There are just seven dairies in the world licensed to make Blue Stilton cheese.

🐑 A total of 85% of women who responded to a British Cheese Board survey experienced bizarre dreams after eating Stilton cheese. These included tales of talking soft toys, dinner party guests being traded for camels and a vegetarian crocodile upset because it could not eat children.

🐑 In north-west England, mushy peas are commonly served with two fried eggs on top as a late-night snack.

🐑 The average British person will eat 550 chickens and other poultry, thirty-six pigs, thirty-six sheep and eight cows in the course of a lifetime.

🐑 Bird's Eye originally planned to launch frozen herring sticks rather than frozen cod sticks, as during the 1950s there was a plentiful supply of cheap British herring. However, after trials found the herring sticks had too many bones for most people, they decided to launch their second-choice instead: cod fish fingers.

🐑 When Captain Bird's Eye was dropped from the famous fish-finger adverts in 1971, *The Times* newspaper ran an obituary. He was brought back to life in 1974.

There is archaeological evidence that an alcoholic drink was made in Scotland 6,000 years ago.

In 1835, a fish curer named Mr Bishop from Great Yarmouth discovered a quantity of fresh herrings had been missed and not processed. To avoid wasting these fish, Bishop is said to have covered them in salt, spitted them and hung them up in the smokehouse. On his return the next morning he was amazed by their colour and taste and so proceeded to perfect the cure, and the Yarmouth Bloater was born

Walker's crisps began life in 1945 when the Leicester-based butcher Henry Walker began selling slices of cooked potato due to a scarcity of meat.

GREAT BRITISH ICONS

The first four British post boxes were introduced as an experiment in St Helier in Jersey on 23 November 1852, following a suggestion from the Surveyor's Clerk, Anthony Trollope, who went on to become one of the most successful and respected authors of the Victorian era.

Each of the London Eye's thirty-two capsules weighs 9.8 tons (10 tonnes).

On a clear day you can see for 25 miles (40 km) from the top of the London Eye.

The crime that led Robin of Loxley, better known as Robin Hood, to become Sherwood Forest's most famous outlaw was poaching deer. At that time, the deer in a royal forest belonged to the King, and killing one of the King's deer was therefore treason, punishable by death.

🐾 British bulldog puppies are often delivered by Caesarean section, as their large heads mean they can get stuck in the birth canal.

🐾 The first fish and chip shop is believed to have been opened by Joseph Malin, a Jewish immigrant from Eastern Europe, in 1860. His business, in London's East End, sold fried fish alongside chipped potatoes, which, until then, had been found only in Irish potato shops.

🐾 Scotland's national drink, whisky, is known in Gaelic as 'uisge beatha', meaning 'water of life'.

🐾 The Ironbridge in Coalbrookdale, Shropshire, was the first cast-iron bridge ever built. It was made from 1,737 individual iron castings that were all fixed together by hand.

🐾 Following the failure of the Gunpowder Plot in 1605, Guy Fawkes was sentenced to be hung, drawn and quartered. However, when he came to be hanged until almost dead at the Old Palace Yard, Westminster, he jumped from the gallows, his neck broke and he died – thereby avoiding the gruesome, later part of the execution.

🐾 Popularised by Charlie Chaplin and Prime Minister Stanley Baldwin, the bowler hat was originally regarded as an informal alternative to the top hat.

🐾 The average Scottish kilt is made of 8 yd (7.3 m) of material and weighs around 5 lb (2.3 kg).

To date, the first and only tartan to make it to the Moon is the Macbean. It was worn by Alan Bean on Apollo 12 in November 1969.

Although Punch and Judy are regarded as part of British seaside tradition, Mr Punch was actually descended from Pulcinella, one of the comic characters from the famous Italian 'Commedia dell' Arte' troupes of travelling players. He was the star puppet in the show *Signor Bologna*, which Samuel Pepys saw in Covent Garden in 1662.

The oldest tartan is the Falkirk tartan, which dates to around AD 260 and was discovered in a jar of coins near Falkirk.

During the 1960s, the mini skirt, popularised by British designer Mary Quant, was often cut 7–8 inches (17.8–20.3 cm) above the knee.

The first post box in mainland Britain was erected in September 1853 in Botchergate, Carlisle. It was octagonal and painted green.

When Edward Elgar wrote the music to what was to become 'Land of Hope and Glory', he had no intention of setting words to it. The idea was first put to him by King Edward VII some months after the premiere of the orchestral version, by which time the march itself had become popular.

Sir Alec Issigonis came up with the design for the Mini after his employers, Morris, asked him to design an efficient small car to help save on fuel following the Suez Crisis of 1956.

Blackpool Tower is lit by 10,000 bulbs during the resort's illuminations.

The 26,000 tons (26,417 tonnes) of steel and iron that make up the Tower are evenly distributed, so if it collapsed it would fall into the sea.

The Blackpool Tower Ballroom floor measures 120 ft by 102 ft (36.6 m by 31.1 m). It comprises 30,602 separate blocks of mahogany, oak and walnut.

Among the Ballroom's one-time strict rules were 'Gentlemen may not dance unless with a lady' and 'Disorderly conduct means immediate expulsion'.

The Domesday Book got its name from the probing and irreversible nature of the information collected, which led people to compare it to the Last Judgement, or 'Doomsday'. Described in the Bible, it referred to the deeds of Christians, which were written in the Book of Life and placed before God for judgement. The name, however, was not adopted until the late 12th century.

It has been estimated that the construction of Stonehenge required more than 30 million hours of labour.

Among the artefacts found buried at Stonehenge have been a woman's torso and a deformed dog's head.

Anthony Gormley's *Angel of the North*, which overlooks the A1 at Gateshead on the southern approach to Tyneside, is seen by at least 90,000 motorists every day.

Although he is the patron saint of Ireland, St Patrick was actually born into a wealthy British family.

Despite being synonymous with Scotland, bagpipes did not originate there. They are believed to have been used in both ancient Egypt and by the Roman infantry before making their way north of the border.

Sir Giles Gilbert Scott, who designed the red telephone box, was also responsible for designing Liverpool's Anglican Cathedral.

Studies have found that Brits prefer to drink their cup of tea when it is between 56 and 60 degrees Celsius (132.8–140 degrees Fahrenheit) – warm but not hot.

As a nation, we drink a massive 165 million cups of tea every day.

According to the Tea Council, 96% of all cups of tea drunk daily in the UK are brewed from tea bags, with 98% of people taking their tea with milk and only 30% taking sugar in tea.

GREAT BRITISH
LAWS

In Anglo-Saxon times, a man could divorce his wife on the grounds that she was too passionate.

It is legal for a male to urinate in public, as long it is on the rear wheel of his motor vehicle and his right hand is on the vehicle.

The Sumptuary Act of Edward III, which was passed in 1336, forbade any person to eat more than two courses in one meal. The Act included the clarification that soup was a full course and not just a sauce.

Betting, gambling, using violent, abusive or obscene language, or behaving in a disorderly manner in a library carries a £200 fine under the 1898 Library Offences Act.

The Loch Ness Monster is named as a protected species under the 1912 Scottish Protection of Animals Act.

You cannot libel a dead person.

It is illegal for a bed to be hung out of a window.

Under an 1888 law, every cyclist in the country had to ring the bell on their bicycle non-stop while they were moving. The law was not abolished until 1930.

Under the UK's Tax Avoidance Schemes Regulations 2006, it is illegal not to tell the taxman anything you do not want him to know, but legal not to tell him information you do not mind him knowing.

It is illegal to enter the Houses of Parliament wearing a suit of armour.

Until 1959, it was illegal not to celebrate Bonfire Night in Britain.

It is still an offence to beat or shake any carpet rug or mat in any street in the Metropolitan Police District, although you are allowed to shake a doormat before 8am.

In Lancashire, no person is permitted to incite a dog to bark after being asked to stop by a constable on the seashore.

The 1830 Beer Shop Act allowed anyone whose name was on the rate books to brew and sell beer in their house.

Taxi drivers are required to ask all passengers if they have smallpox or the plague.

In Liverpool, it is illegal for a woman to be topless in public unless she is a clerk in a tropical fish store.

Under the Stocks Act of 1405, every parish that runs its own affairs should have a set of stocks. If you are a village and don't have a set, your village should be downgraded to a hamlet.

After the 1745 Jacobite rebellion, which saw the defeat of the Highland clans who had backed Bonnie Prince Charlie, tartan and the kilt were banned by the Government, who were fearful of a repeat of the rebellion. The law was repealed in 1782.

Under a law enacted by Edward VI, any person found breaking a boiled egg at the sharp end would be sentenced to twenty-four hours in the village stocks.

If you shoot a fowl and it lands on your neighbour's land, you are not allowed to fetch it without permission, but it is legal to send your dog over to fetch it.

In Norman times, a person found guilty of slander had not only to pay damages to the injured party, but also stand in the market place of their nearest town and, while holding their nose between two fingers, declare themselves to be a liar.

You can be fined for having a number plate in italics.

Under a 13th-century British law, any baker caught selling underweight bread would face the pillory. It is said that bakers began making an extra loaf to ensure that they were never short, hence the phrase 'a baker's dozen'.

The age of consent in Britain was set at twelve in 1275, and remained so until 1885, when it was raised to sixteen.

Under the Metropolitan Streets Act of 1867, people are prohibited from driving cattle through the streets of London between the hours of 10am and 7pm. The maximum penalty is a £25 fine for each head of cattle.

Until 1976, taxi drivers were required by law to carry a bale of hay to feed a horse.

Under Henry II, anyone found killing, wounding or maiming fairies could face the death penalty.

Under the Wildlife and Countryside Act 1981, it is an offence to 'intentionally take, damage or destroy' a wild bird's nest. That also includes intentionally destroying or taking down a nest that has been built in or onto your own house.

In 1436, the first of two laws limiting trade in grain was passed. The aim of the Corn Laws was to make Britain self-sufficient in grain through the restriction of imports and exports. It led to widespread starvation as the price of grain rocketed.

In medieval England, it was illegal to stand near the monarch when not wearing socks.

In 1393, King Richard II passed an Act making it compulsory for pubs and inns to have a sign, in order to identify them to the official Ale Taster. This proved to be particularly useful for a population who were largely illiterate.

It is still illegal for cabbies to carry rabid dogs or corpses.

Under a 17th-century law, it is illegal to fly a Union Jack from a British boat. The law was brought in to prevent civilian ships from attempting to avoid harbour charges, by pretending to be naval vessels.

The 1857 Matrimonial Causes Act allowed divorce through the law courts. Before this time, it had required an Act of Parliament and cost at least £700. Under the terms of the Act, the husband only had to prove his wife's adultery. The wife, however, had to prove her husband had committed not just adultery but *also* either incest, bigamy, cruelty or desertion.

In London, it is illegal to flag down a taxi if you have the plague.

Any boy under the age of ten may not see a naked mannequin.

Under the Anatomy Act of 1540, every year schools of anatomy were given the corpses of four individuals who had been executed to practise on.

Londoners are not allowed to keep a pigsty in the front of their homes.

In 1647, the English parliament passed a law that made Christmas illegal. Festivities were banned by Oliver Cromwell, a Puritan, who considered it immoral to have feasting and revelry on what was supposed to be a holy day. The ban was lifted in 1660, two years after his death.

Throughout the whole of England it is illegal to eat mince pies on 25 December.

Until 1929 in Scotland, it was possible for boys to get married at fourteen and girls at twelve years old with or without parental consent.

The Isle of Man retained the death penalty for murder until 1991, although the last execution to take place on the island was in the 19th century.

In 16th-century England, it was made illegal to bury the dead in linen shrouds, as linen was in short supply and was required to make paper.

In Scotland, it is illegal to be drunk while in possession of a cow.

The Metropolitan Police Act of 1839 banned the firing of a cannon close to a dwelling house.

The Devon and Cornwall Seashore Act of 1609 allows any resident of the two counties to take sand 'under the full sea-mark' to improve the quality of their soil.

Until 1835, anyone who had a trade in the City of London had to be made a Freeman of the City. Those who carried the title were allowed to take a flock of sheep across London Bridge without being charged a toll and also to drive geese down Cheapside. They could also gain immunity from press ganging, get married in St Paul's and would not be arrested if found drunk and disorderly.

A pregnant woman can legally relieve herself anywhere she wants, even – if she requests – in a policeman's helmet.

It is illegal to die in the Houses of Parliament.

In England, all men over the age of fourteen must carry out two hours of longbow practice a day.

You can shoot a Welsh person at any time during the day on a Sunday, as long as it is with a longbow, in the Cathedral Close in Hereford.

Meanwhile, an ancient law says Welsh people can be shot with a bow and arrow inside the city walls and after midnight in Chester.

In the 16th century, a man could be fined for not wearing a wool cap.

UK law states that any new drug must be tested on at least two different species of live mammal, one of which must be a large non-rodent.

It is illegal for a lady to eat chocolates on a public conveyance.

It is illegal to be drunk on licensed premises.

It is an act of treason to place a postage stamp bearing the British king or queen's image upside down.

Homosexuality was legalised in England and Wales in 1967 but remained against the law in Scotland until 1980.

Under the Profane Oaths Act of 1745, labourers and common soldiers, seamen, and sailors found guilty of swearing were fined one shilling, while 'every other person, under the degree of gentleman' was fined two shillings, with gentlemen and those of even higher social standing facing a five-shilling penalty. The fines were doubled for a second offence and trebled for a third.

Royal Navy ships that enter the Port of London are still required to provide a barrel of rum to the Constable of the Tower of London.

The head of any dead whale found on the British coast automatically becomes the property of the King, while the tail become the property of the Queen (in case she needs the bones for her corset).

Under the 1847 Town Police Clauses Act, making bonfires, flying kites, sliding on ice or snow, extinguishing any lamp, or wilfully and wantonly disturbing residents by ringing their doorbells are all punishable with a £1,000 fine.

A 19th-century British law stipulated that those who successfully committed suicide would be executed.

In the city of York, it is legal to murder a Scotsman within the ancient city walls, but only if he is carrying a bow and arrow.

Under an 1865 law, any self-propelled vehicle on an English highway had to have a crew of three, one of whom had to walk in front of the carriage with a red flag to warn horse-drawn vehicles that it was approaching.

In England, juries are composed of twelve people. In Scotland it is fifteen.

Police are not required to clean up a crime scene once evidence has been gathered.

The 1979 film *Monty Python's Life of Brian* was banned for blasphemy by the local council of Runnymede, until it was pointed out that they did not have any cinemas in their jurisdiction.

Under English Common Law, if you are owed money, you can accept anything to settle the debt, except for a lesser amount of money.

GREAT BRITISH SUPERSTITIONS AND TRADITIONS

Old Scottish folklore held that a bride would have bad luck if she met a priest, a monk or a hare on the way to church, and good luck if a spider, toad, cat or wolf crossed her path.

Meanwhile, in the north-east of Scotland, a chamber pot full of salt was once a common wedding present for the happy couple.

If you take a candle to church at Christmas in Wales, don't bring it home. Instead, blow it out and leave it there with the vicar for good luck.

During the 19th century, many people believed that hot cross buns baked on Good Friday would not go mouldy and had special healing powers. It was thought they could be used as a cure for medical complaints such as indigestion and some people even grated fossilised remains of the Easter treat on to wounds to help them heal.

One in four British people believes that wearing lucky knickers brings good fortune.

If a bee enters your home, it is said to be a sign that you will soon have a visitor. If you kill the bee, you will have bad luck or the visitor will be unpleasant.

When a cuckoo is seen for the first time of the year in Guernsey, you should put a stone on your head and run as fast as you can until the stone falls off. You should then mark the spot where the stone fell and return to it the following day. There should be money underneath it.

During the early 16th century, a visitor to a home in England would always kiss the family cat to bring good luck.

In Wales, families would try to repay all debts and push the bank balance into the black before a New Year. Tradition stated that ending a year in debt would mean a whole new year of debt.

In Scotland, it was the custom for the builder of a boat to hide a gold coin somewhere in the keel. The purpose of the gold coin was to bring good fortune. The hiding place was known only to the builder, and never to the ship's owner.

It was once believed that if someone else could count your teeth when you yawned you would lose a year of your life, so you covered your mouth to hide them.

The spouse who goes to sleep first on his or her wedding day will be the first to die.

When first boarding a ship, it is said to be unlucky to step forward with the left foot first. However, it is much worse if you also sneeze to the left while doing so.

In many of Britain's coastal towns it has long been common to see a piece of seaweed hung outside the door to predict the following day's weather. This is because fresh seaweed is hygroscopic – meaning it will absorb moisture from the atmosphere. So if the atmosphere is damp, as it is before rain, the seaweed will become supple and wet.

In the Highlands of Scotland, it was thought that a child born early in the morning had a better chance of survival. The saying was, 'The later the hour, the shorter the life.' Traditionally, a newborn baby would swallow fresh butter to protect against fairies. It would also be presented with a newly laid egg, a piece of bread and a pinch of salt, to ensure that it would always have the essentials of life.

Another Highlands superstition was that a grave dug on a Sunday would lead to another being dug for a family member before the week was out.

If a lady's apron suddenly falls off for no apparent reason, it is said that she will have a baby within a year.

It is said that a man with a hairy chest is a better lover than one without.

The appearance of bubbles on top of your cup of tea can mean that you are in for some money.

It is unlucky to cut your fingernails on either Friday or Sunday; however, if you cut them before breakfast on Monday morning you will receive a present before the week is out.

Calendars that are received at Christmas should never be hung on the wall until the start of the New Year.

An old superstition to get rid of warts was to rub them with a peeled apple and then feed the apple to a pig.

During the 1930s, women were warned not to sit on a bed in which a baby had recently been born, or they would also become pregnant in the near future.

In 19th-century Scotland, people would always keep a close eye on a newborn baby's hands. If they kept their hands closed, it was said to be a sign that they would keep hold of all money that came their way. Should their hands remained open, the money would go as fast as it came.

The Scots believe that if a beetle enters the room while your family are seated, you will experience bad luck. However, that bad luck will turn into even greater misfortune if you should kill the beetle.

Welsh folklore has it that if you see a fox on its own, then good luck is in store; however, if a pack of foxes should cross your path, then trouble is on its way.

If you pick a pansy when the weather is particularly good, then you will bring on rain before too long.

In the north of England it is believed that if you wear a sprig of rosemary in your buttonhole, you will be successful in everything you do. It is said to particularly help improve your memory.

If you hiccup, someone is thinking about you.

In some rural parts of the country, many believe that you should not reply 'very well' when someone enquires about your health. Instead, you should always qualify it, or else you could be in trouble.

A pimple on the tongue is said to show that a person has been telling lies.

In 19th-century England, it was considered disrespectful to point at the moon.

In Wales, if anyone sitting around a fireplace on Christmas Day casts a shadow with his or her head, it is said that they will die during the coming year.

In certain parts of Britain, it is believed that eating the tongue of a dog will cure all ulcers.

A girl can apparently tell what kind of man her future husband is going to be by the kind of bird she first sees on Valentine's Day. A blackbird is said to indicate a clergyman; a sparrow means a farmer; a dove – a good man; a goldfinch – a rich man; and a robin – a sailor.

If a steeplejack ties a knot in his braces, he is said to be protected from having an accident, as the ancient symbol of the knot signifies safety and security.

Some rural tradesmen believe that one of the coins given by the first customer of the day should always be returned to ensure a successful day's trading.

If a thread knots while it is being used, then the seamstress will soon argue with someone.

If a bride sees a lizard on the way to the church, then her marriage will be an unhappy one.

If you see your cat or dog eating grass, then rain will be in imminent.

Many people say that dimples are lucky because they believe the mark was made by the impression of God's finger.

During the 19th century, it was believed that tumours, swellings, and other skin problems could be cured by stroking the affected area with a dead man's hand. Hangmen would often charge people for the use of a hand following a public hanging.

It is unlucky to be a bridesmaid three times. If you are, you need to make sure you are asked a further four times, otherwise you will never marry.

In the 16th century, it was believed that asthma could be cured by eating the foam from a mule's mouth.

An ancient British superstition says that carrying an acorn about your person will stop you growing old.

During the early 20th century, you were told that should an eyelash fall out, you must put it on the back of your hand and make a wish, and that wish will come true.

If sage grows in abundance in your garden, then the woman who lives there is said to be very strong willed.

A silk ribbon around the neck is believed to prevent disease.

If a ladybird lands on you, you must count the number of spots on its back, as each one represents a happy month to come.

A live cockerel was often killed as a cure for epilepsy in Scotland and Ireland.

If you have any ornaments in your house, you should always have the face of the ornament facing the door by which people enter the room. It is unlucky if they are not facing that way.

During the 1940s, children would always inspect the serial number on their bus ticket. If the numbers added up to twenty-one, the ticket was thought to be lucky and was saved.

If a drinking glass is accidentally struck and makes a ringing sound, you must stop the sound immediately or else a sailor at sea will be drowned.

Horseshoes that have been found by their owner are believed to be ten times more lucky than those that are acquired in other ways, while those that are bought are not meant to be lucky at all.

If you suffer from cramp, you should place a bowl of water under your bed.

If you see a spider at night, it is a sign that you will have a letter in the morning.

In Devon, it was believed that if, as a married couple leaves the church, the bride puts her foot outside the church door before her husband, then she will be the boss.

It is said if two people use the same water to wash their hands – either together or one after the other – they would soon quarrel.

During the start of the 20th century, it was thought that if a woman's petticoat hung below her dress then her father liked her more than her mother.

Past cures for chilblains have included thrashing them with holly, rubbing them with snow, and bathing them in urine, as long as that urine was fresh and your own.

Warts can be cured by stealing bread, rubbing it on the wart, and then burying it.

Putting your stockings on the left leg first was said to be a way of preventing rheumatism.

It is said to be bad luck for an actor to whistle in the dressing room or backstage. Anyone who does whistle must go out of the dressing room, turn round three times, then knock on the door and ask for permission to be admitted.

Victorians believed that if the head of a bed was placed towards the north it foretold a short life; towards the south meant a long life; to the east meant you would receive riches; while having the head of the bed towards the west would lead to travel.

You should never give someone a knife, pair of scissors, or any other sharp object as a gift. Instead, they must always pay for it with some small token.

If you let someone else pick up your comb after you have dropped it, you will have a surprise.

It was often thought in Ireland and Scotland that the last person to be buried in a graveyard had to watch over all those already buried, until the next funeral took place. This would often lead to fights between rival funeral parties determined that their deceased loved one should not have to take on the onerous task.

The most widely held superstitious belief in Britain is touching wood, followed by crossing fingers, not walking under ladders, fear of breaking a mirror, being worried about the number thirteen and carrying a lucky charm.

A study by the University of Hertfordshire found that the Scots are the most superstitious people in Britain, followed by the English, Welsh, and Northern Irish. Women are more superstitious than men and youngsters are more superstitious than old people.

... and one-quarter of Brits would not consider buying a house if it was number 13.

Football manager Harry Redknapp wore the same shirt, tie, pants and jacket during a twenty-match unbeaten run while in charge at Bournemouth.

Chelsea and England footballer John Terry is so superstitious he follows a whole series of rituals before every match. These include always having the same seat on the team bus, tying tape around his socks three times, cutting tubular grip for his shin-pads the same size every game, and parking in the same space in Chelsea's underground car park at Stamford Bridge.

GREAT BRITISH WRITERS

 Charles Dickens was an insomniac and always slept in a bed facing north because he believed it would give him a better chance of getting some sleep.

 Dickens wrote *Oliver Twist* because he wanted to expose the ill treatment of children in contemporary society.

 Little Larry, Puny Pete and Small Sam were alternative names that Dickens considered for the character that was to become Tiny Tim.

 John Bunyan, author of *The Pilgrim's Progress*, wrote most of his famous book while in jail. He was imprisoned for twelve years for preaching without a licence.

 Diarist Samuel Pepys wrote in a special code that was not translated until the 19th century.

In 1907, Rudyard Kipling, author of *The Jungle Book*, became the first British winner of the Nobel Prize for Literature. It was given 'in consideration of the power of observation, originality of imagination, virility of ideas and remarkable talent for narration'.

The Wind in the Willows author Kenneth Grahame wanted to go to university after finishing school, but due to lack of family money had to abandon plans and went to work at the Bank of England instead. It was not a bad move. He had become Secretary of the Bank by the age of thirty-eight.

William Shakespeare invented the word 'assassination'.

When Shakespeare died, he left most of his property to Susanna, his first child, and not to his wife Anne Hathaway. Instead, his loyal wife received his 'second best bed'. This wasn't too bad, however, as it was his marriage bed. His best bed was for guests.

Shakespeare never published any of his plays. It was his fellow actors John Hemminges and Henry Condell who posthumously recorded his work as a dedication to him in 1623, publishing thirty-six of his plays. This collection, known as *The First Folio*, is the source from which all published Shakespeare books are derived and is said to be important proof that he authored his plays.

Shakespeare spelled his surname eleven different ways.

Hamlet has the most lines in a single Shakespeare play, with 1,422.

Jane Austen's *Northanger Abbey* was originally rejected by publishers, as was H.G. Wells's *The Time Machine* and Kenneth Grahame's *The Wind in the Willows*.

Peter Pan creator J.M. Barrie used to buy Brussels sprouts every day. When this was commented on by a friend, Barrie reportedly explained, 'I cannot resist ordering them. The words are so lovely to say.'

T.E. Lawrence left his manuscript of *Seven Pillars of Wisdom* in the cafe at Reading station. He called the station from Oxford when he arrived, but the case containing the work had gone and was never found. The version that was eventually published was an earlier one, which Lawrence regarded as inferior.

J.K. Rowling was advised to use her initials rather than her first name on the cover of her books, as boys were not keen on buying books written by female authors.

Dylan Thomas's highly acclaimed first volume of poetry, *18 Poems*, was published in 1934 when he was just twenty.

In 1945, science-fiction writer Arthur C. Clarke published a paper in which he predicted that, at 22,000 miles (35,400 km) above the Earth's surface, communications satellites would sit in geo-stationary orbit, allowing electronic signals to be bounced off them around the globe. Although the comment was largely ignored at the time, the first satellite was placed into geo-stationary orbit in 1964, just nineteen years after Clarke's prediction.

William Caxton's *Recuyell of the Historyes of Troye*, based on a novel by a Frenchman, was the first book printed in the English language in around 1474, although it was printed in Bruges.

Geoffrey Chaucer's *Canterbury Tales* is believed to be the first book in English that was actually printed in England, in 1477.

American publishers Dial Press rejected George Orwell's political satire *Animal Farm* on the grounds that it was 'impossible to sell animal stories in the USA'.

Author and playwright Alan Bennett does not own a computer.

Charles Dickens's public readings of his books were so effective that members of the audience would often faint during the murder scene in *Oliver Twist*.

British writer Alice Porlock published her first book, *Portrait of My Victorian Youth,* when she was 102 years old.

Although regarded as one of the greatest poets of his generation, only five of war poet Wilfred Owen's poems were published before his death.

The 'J.R.R.' in *Lord of the Rings* author Tolkein's name stands for John Roland Ruel, while the 'C.S.' in *The Lion, the Witch and the Wardrobe* creator Lewis's name stands for Clive Staples.

Discworld author Terry Pratchett sold his first story when he was thirteen. It earned him enough money to buy a second-hand typewriter.

Anna Sewell's 1877 novel *Black Beauty* is noted for having created a huge change in attitude towards the treatment of working animals, in particular for the more humane treatment of horses.

When Sewell was fourteen, she was injured in an accident but received improper treatment, which meant she could never walk properly again. She began to rely heavily on horses to pull her around in a cart, which allowed her some freedom of movement, and she soon grew to love them.

Much of the real Watership Down, the setting for Richard Adams's famous novel of the same name, is owned by Lord Andrew Lloyd Webber.

Before making it big with *Bridget Jones's Diary*, writer Helen Fielding's first attempt at romance writing was rejected by Mills & Boon.

Enid Blyton could write 10,000 words in one day.

England's first female novelist was Aphra Behn, who published her novel *Oroonoko* in 1688 about an African prince who is made a slave. Some people at the time did not believe that a woman was capable of writing so well, and accused her of plagiarism.

Twenty-six per cent of all books sold in the UK in 2007 were those recommended by Richard and Judy's Book Club.

Wuthering Heights was Emily Brontë's only novel.

Emily, Anne and Charlotte Brontë would have been called Prunty, had their father not changed the family name, having been inspired by the Sicilian Dukedom of Bronte awarded to Admiral Nelson.

Enid Blyton wrote 600 children's stories.

Blyton's real name was Daryl Walters.

A book on the future of fromage frais pots won the 2009 award for the strangest title of the year. *The 2009-2014 World Outlook for 60-milligram Containers of Fromage Frais* by Professor Philip M. Parker won The Diagram Prize, with *Baboon Metaphysics* by Dorothy L. Cheney and Robert M. Seyfarth coming second and *Curbside Consultation of the Colon* by Brooks D. Cash taking third.

Author Libby Rees, who was born in 1995, was just nine years old when she wrote her first published book, *Help, Hope and Happiness*.

Women's rights campaigner Marie Stopes attempted to have her first book, *Married Life*, published during World War I. One publisher however, not happy with a book that argued marriage should be an equal relationship between husband and wife, replied, 'There will be few enough men for the girls to marry; and a book like this would frighten off the few.'

Best-selling author Jilly Cooper still writes her novels on a typewriter she calls 'Monica'.

In 1970, Cooper took the only copy of the manuscript of her novel *Riders* with her when she went out to lunch, only to leave it on a London bus. She never found it, and did not finish rewriting the book for another twenty-four years.

A 2009 survey for World Book Day revealed the book British people are most likely to have lied about reading is *Nineteen Eighty-Four* by George Orwell.

The name of James Bond villain Blofeld was inspired by the English cricket commentator Henry Blofeld's father, with whom Bond author Ian Fleming went to school.

Fleming named James Bond himself after an American ornithologist and author of *Birds of the West Indies*. Actor Pierce Brosnan can be seen reading the book in the 007 film *Die Another Day*.

D.H. Lawrence's novel *Lady Chatterley's Lover* was banned for obscenity for over thirty years.

When the Church of England clergyman Rev. W. Awdry began to achieve fame as the author of the *Thomas the Tank Engine* books, the press dubbed him 'the Puff Puff Parson'.

Salman Rushdie, author of *The Satanic Verses*, came up with the 'naughty but nice' slogan to advertise fresh cream cakes.

When renowned children's author Roald Dahl was fifteen, his English teacher wrote in his report that he seemed 'incapable of marshalling his thought on paper'.

Following the death of her husband Percy Shelley in 1822, *Frankenstein* author Mary Shelley salvaged what was left of his heart during his cremation. Following her own death, the heart was discovered, wrapped in silk, between the pages of *Adonis*, having remained in her travelling desk for almost thirty years.

The original title of Jane Austen's novel *Pride and Prejudice* was 'First Impression'. The book was originally published in 1813, seventeen years after she started writing it.

The 17th-century poet Thomas May died after being strangled by the cloth he used to support his double chin.

The first *Mr Men* book written by Roger Hargreaves was *Mr Tickle*. He was created after his son Adam asked his father what a tickle looked like. Hargreaves drew a figure with a round orange body and long, rubbery arms.

The ten most borrowed authors from British libraries (as of 2008) are: 1 – James Patterson, 2 – Jacqueline Wilson, 3 – Daisy Meadows, 4 – Nora Roberts, 5 – Francesca Simon, 6 – Mick Inkpen, 7 – Jospehine Cox, 8 – Danielle Steel, 9 – Janet and Allan Ahlberg, 10 – Ian Whybrow.

Robert Louis Stevenson's best-seller *Treasure Island* was originally called 'The Sea Cook'.

George Eliot submitted her second novel under the title 'Sister Maggie', but her publisher, John Blackwood, did not like the title and told her to call it *The Mill on the Floss* instead.

After getting married in the early 1970s, Tony and Maureen Wheeler decided to set off on an overland adventure from London to Sydney via Europe and Asia. They took in places that were not well travelled by Westerners at the time, such as Iran, Turkey and India. Eventually, the pair arrived in Sydney with 27 cents to their name. When people began asking them about the places they had been to and where they had stayed, they decided to write everything down in a book. It became the first *Lonely Planet* guide.

Edward Lear, best known for his nonsense poems such as *The Owl and the Pussycat*, was the youngest of twenty-one children.

Lear was so devoted to his cat Foss (the subject of many of his rhymes, jokes and drawings), that when building work near his home on the Italian Riviera disturbed his peace and prompted him to move, he had an identical house built elsewhere so that Foss could find his way about.

Harry Potter books were always released on a Saturday to stop children taking a day off school to read them.

William Blake's poem 'Jerusalem' was actually just part of the preface to a long epic poem entitled *Milton*. Although composed between 1804 and 1808, it was not well known until World War I, when it was published in an anthology of nationalist verse, and after proving very popular, was set to music by Sir Hubert Parry in 1916.

The UK's most borrowed book is Patricia Cornwell's *At Risk* – although the author's combined loans only put her at number twenty-one in the overall list.

Roald Dahl wrote most of his books in a shed, which he called his 'hut'.

Before becoming a full-time poet, *Under Milk Wood* author Dylan Thomas worked as a news reporter on the *South Wales Daily Post* in Swansea. He was not particularly good at his job, however, often getting facts wrong, failing to show up to cover events and preferring instead to loiter at the local snooker hall.

Dr Samuel Johnson took eight years to write the first comprehensive dictionary.

Johnson left Oxford University without gaining a degree.

He wrote his book *Rasselas* in just one week, in order to pay for his mother's funeral.

On the other hand, it took Peter Roget a massive forty-seven years to complete his *Thesaurus of English Words and Phrases*.

Jane Austen's *Pride and Prejudice* was originally published in three volumes.

Before being commissioned to create what was to become *The Guinness Book of Records*, twins Norris and Ross McWhirter had worked as sports journalists and also ran an agency in London supplying facts and figures to Fleet Street newspapers.

Guinness World Records receives 60,000 applications a year from around the globe to break or set a new record. Not all are accepted as some are not measurable, not standardisable, not breakable, too specific or not enough of a challenge. Only 4,000 records are published in the book each year.

Far from the Madding Crowd author Thomas Hardy took the title of his novel from a line in an 18th-century poem by Thomas Gray entitled 'Elegy in a Country Churchyard'.

There are only six known signatures by William Shakespeare in existence. Three of the six appear on his will.

The walrus in Lewis Carroll's 1871 poem *The Walrus and the Carpenter* was inspired by a stuffed specimen in Sunderland Museum.

More than 400 biographies of Charlie Chaplin have been written.

John Milton was paid only £10 for the copyright to his masterpiece *Paradise Lost*.

Robert Burns only published his first book of poetry, *Poems, Chiefly in the Scottish Dialect*, in 1786, to raise money for a boat ticket to Jamaica, where he was to emigrate and become a bookkeeper – leaving behind his life of poverty and pregnant mistresses. The book did so well that he became both rich and famous. He decided to stay.

Robert Louis Stevenson was paid £100 (£8,500 in today's money) by his publishers for *Treasure Island*.

Alice in Wonderland author Lewis Carroll had a stammer.

One night in 1798, poet Samuel Taylor Coleridge fell asleep in his chair while reading. During three hours of deep sleep, he 'composed' between two and three hundred lines of poetry. After awakening, he had written down just fifty-four lines of 'Kubla Khan' when he was interrupted by a visitor. Later, when Coleridge returned to his desk, he found that he could no longer remember his dream poem.

When Beatrix Potter was fifteen, she began to keep a journal that she wrote in a secret code. It was so complex that when she read back over it in later life, she found it difficult to understand herself. It was not until fifteen years after her death that the code was finally cracked.

Eric Blair took the pen name George Orwell from the River Orwell in Suffolk.

A mythical Devon dog, 'the hound of Dartmoor', inspired Arthur Conan Doyle to write the Sherlock Holmes mystery *The Hound of the Baskervilles*.

Brideshead Revisited author Evelyn Waugh was a schoolteacher before turning his attention to writing. During his first teaching job he attempted suicide by swimming out to sea, but turned back to shore after being stung by jellyfish.

When J.K. Rowling published her first Harry Potter novel, her publishers warned her that she would never make any money out of children's books.

J.K. Rowling makes £5 every second.

Charles Dickens created 989 named characters.

Before writing *The Hitchhiker's Guide to the Galaxy*, Douglas Adams worked as a script editor on *Doctor Who*, during the period when Tom Baker was in charge of the TARDIS. Adams is credited with bringing the Baker Doctor's surreal humour into the show.

Poet Lord Byron kept a bear while at Cambridge University because dogs were not allowed.

During the seven years he was Poet Laureate, William Wordsworth did not write any poems.

Before becoming a full-time children's author, *Tracey Beaker* creator Jacqueline Wilson worked for a magazine publisher, where she helped found *Jackie* magazine. She admitted in an interview that it was actually named after her.

In all, 100 million copies of J.R.R. Tolkein's *The Lord of the Rings* trilogy have been sold.

Dame Barbara Cartland had written an estimated 723 novels by the time she died, aged ninety-eight, in 2000.

Cartland was often nicknamed 'The Animated Meringue'.

Roald Dahl wrote the screenplay for both *Chitty Chitty Bang Bang* and the Bond film *You Only Live Twice*.

Rudyard Kipling turned down the post of Poet Laureate, although he did accept the Nobel Prize for Literature in 1907.

In his will, Charles Dickens asked to be buried in an inexpensive, unostentatious and extremely private manner. In fact, he was buried in Westminster Abbey.

Dickens based the school in *Nicholas Nickleby* on William Shaw's establishment in Yorkshire. After the book was published, Shaw was ruined.

After J.K. Rowling won the Smarties Book Prize for children's fiction for the third year running for *Harry Potter and the Prisoner of Azkaban*, she asked for further Harry Potter books not to be considered for the prize.

William Wordsworth and Alfred, Lord Tennyson both borrowed the same suit from their fellow poet, Samuel Rogers, when they went to Buckingham Palace to be invested as Poet Laureate.

A Mills & Boon book is sold in the UK every three seconds.

Ten million books are sold each year in the UK, of which over 7 million are romance novels.

Winnie the Pooh creator A.A. Milne was responsible for adapting Kenneth Grahame's *The Wind in the Willows* when it was put on the stage under the title *Toad of Toad Hall*.

John Milton completed his most famous work, *Paradise Lost,* in 1664 when he was fifty-six. Milton, who was blind, composed the entire work over the course of six years.

When Richard Adams's *Watership Down* was first published in 1972, only 2,500 copies were printed. It went on to sell 50 million copies around the world.

In 2003, Gloucestershire Council had to inform its residents that a new £2 million library would not be opening on schedule because they had forgotten to order any books or shelves.

Paperback books were first mass-marketed in 1935 when Allen Lane launched Penguin Books. After a weekend visiting Agatha Christie in Devon, Lane found himself on a platform at Exeter station searching its bookstall for something to read on his journey back to London, but discovered only popular magazines and reprints of Victorian novels. Appalled by the selection on offer, Lane decided that good-quality contemporary fiction should be made available at a reasonable price and sold not only in traditional bookshops, but also in railway stations, tobacconists and chain stores.

Jane Austen never married. She once fell in love, but her suitor could not afford to marry her and moved away.

A 2003 nationwide search by the BBC to find the nation's favourite read revealed that J.R.R. Tolkein's *The Lord of the Rings* was most people's favourite book, followed by *Pride and Prejudice* by Jane Austen, *His Dark Materials* by Philip Pullman, *The Hitchhiker's Guide to the Galaxy* by Douglas Adams, *Harry Potter and the Goblet of Fire* by J.K. Rowling, *To Kill a Mockingbird* by Harper Lee, *Winnie the Pooh* by A.A. Milne, *Nineteen Eighty-Four* by George Orwell, *The Lion, The Witch and the Wardrobe* by C.S. Lewis, and *Jane Eyre* by Charlotte Brontë.

THE GREAT BRITISH PEOPLE

In 2008, the five most popular names for a girl were: Olivia, Ruby, Grace, Emily and Jessica. The five most popular names for a boy were: Jack, Oliver, Harry, Alfie and Charlie.

There were 1,048 babies named Gertrude in 1907, but none in 2005.

A 2009 study found there were people in Britain with the names Terry Bull, Stan Still, Barb Dwyer, Max Power, Justin Case, Mary Christmas and Paige Turner.

The average Brit's savings would last just fifty-two days if he or she found themselves out of work.

People in Yorkshire eat more fish and chips than in any other area of Great Britain.

According to the Potato Council, 10% of the British potato crop is needed to supply the UK's 9,500 fish and chip shops.

A 2008 survey found that British boys cost £7,000 more to rear than girls during school years.

The most popular inquiry at Citizens Advice Bureaux comes from people wanting to change their name.

The average British person spends 1,669 hours working every year.

It is estimated that there are more than 2,000 Esperanto speakers in the UK.

The ten most commonly reported phobias in the UK, according to a survey of its members by Anxiety UK are: social phobia – fear of interacting with other people; agoraphobia – fear of open and public spaces; emetophobia – fear of vomiting; erythrophobia – fear of blushing; driving phobia – fear of driving a car; hypochondria – fear of illness; aerophobia – fear of flying; arachnophobia – fear of spiders; zoophobia – fear of animals; and claustrophobia – fear of confined spaces.

The membership of the National Trust is greater than the population of Wales.

More household accidents happen on a Sunday than any other day, apart from Mothering Sunday. The fewest household accidents occur on a Friday.

The left testicle hangs lower than the right in 85% of men.

The emergency admissions hospital statistics for 2006–07 found that 3,435 people had been injured using power tools, 452 had had lawnmower accidents, sixty people had been struck by lightning, 16,000 had hurt themselves falling out of bed and three people had been bitten or struck by a crocodile or alligator.

Bras are responsible for 400 underwear-related injuries in Britain each year. In 1999, two women were killed in London when a bolt of lightning hit the metal under-wiring in one of their bras, which acted as a conductor.

The most-read Sunday newspaper in this country is the *News of the World*, with *the Sun* the most-read daily.

More than 1,000 Britons lose luggage at airports every day, with lost or stolen baggage second only to medical problems in the number of claims made in 2008.

The average UK household bins £8-worth of leftovers every week.

John Roy from Clacton began growing his moustache in 1939 and by 1976 it was 74.5 inches (189.2 cm) wide. He accidentally sat on it in the bath several years later and lost 16.5 inches (41.9 cm).

The average length of a journey to school is 1.5 miles (2.4 km) among younger children and 3.4 miles (5.4 km) among eleven- to sixteen-year-olds.

The number of divorcing couples hiring private detectives to spy on cheating partners is on the increase. A 2007 survey of divorce lawyers found that 49% of break-ups involved a private detective, compared with just 18% the previous year.

A third of water used in the home goes down the toilet.

In all, 90% of British households own a dictionary, while 80% have a bible and 70% are in possession of a cookery book.

More than 77% of British shoppers say they have not owned up to getting too much change, while 40% of shoppers admit that they have walked out of a shop without paying for goods.

Men in the UK have a life expectancy of 76.23, while for women it is 81.3 years.

The UK has a population density of 650 people per square mile (1,683 people per square kilometre).

British people spend around a year of their lives queuing.

A 2008 study found that Britons spend up to three hours every day wasting time. The survey of 1,600 adults by the Learning and Skills Council showed that most time was wasted waiting for children, partners or colleagues, queuing, gossiping, being stuck in traffic jams or shopping.

The average person in Britain consumes 3,460 calories a day. The recommended calorie intake is 2,000.

The top reason for skiving off work is a hangover. More than 50% of people, however, said they would be less likely to skive if their pay was docked.

According to leading insurers, the most dangerous and high-risk occupations in Britain are: fisherman or merchant seafarers, bomb disposal or mine-clearance expert, oil or gas rigger, construction workers, lorry and commercial driver and deep-sea diver.

A total of 55% of people will yawn within five minutes of seeing someone else yawn.

The average Brit puts on 6lb (2.7 kg) over the Christmas holiday.

A 2008 UK-wide poll, commissioned by Play England found half of seven- to twelve-year-olds have been stopped from climbing trees, while 21% of those surveyed had been banned from playing conkers because their parents were worried about them getting hurt.

The UK has more people aged over sixty than under sixteen.

A 2005 study by the Institute for Public Policy Research estimated that 5.5 million British people live abroad on a permanent basis. Indeed, Britain now has more nationals living abroad than almost any other country.

By 2050, the UK will be paying out £6.5 billion in benefits and £1.3 billion in healthcare costs to UK pensioners overseas.

In all, 16% of smokers have their first cigarette of the day within five minutes of waking up.

There are five times more people aged over 85 than there were in 1951.

The average British employee spends fourteen days a year on personal emails, telephone calls and surfing the Internet.

One in twenty of Britain's population will attend a summer music festival.

The average British woman spends one hour and fourteen minutes every week ironing her family's wardrobe. This equates to a total of two days and 3.5 miles (5.6 km) of material every year.

The average person in Britain sends fifty Christmas cards.

A recent survey found that 'You're Beautiful' by James Blunt is now more popular at weddings than long-time favourite 'Angels' by Robbie Williams. 'Angels' also featured on the top list of songs requested at funerals.

Hampshire builder Graham Parker finally solved his Rubik's cube in 2009, twenty-six years after he bought it. He had spent 27,400 hours working on it, and had suffered back and wrist problems as a result. The fastest time to solve the puzzle is 7.08 seconds.

Jill Piggott and Pete Freeman married in the clothing section of their local Asda in York in February 2004. The couple had met in the store, where the bride worked on the checkout and the groom was a frequent customer. They left the ceremony to a bagpipe version of the Asda tune.

The youngest person to have visited both the North and South Poles is English schoolboy Robert Schumann. He made the trip to the North Pole in 1992, aged ten, and visited the South Pole the following year, aged eleven.

The average British woman spends two years of her life looking in the mirror.

A total of 60% of British school leavers enrol in further education. In Finland the figure is 92%, while in the United States it is 83%.

A quarter of the UK's Catholic population goes to church on a Sunday.

Smith is the most common surname in the UK, followed by Jones, Williams, Taylor, Brown, Davies, Evans, Thomas, Wilson and Johnson.

The most common male name in England and Wales is David Jones, while the most common female name is Margaret Smith.

A 2009 survey by Onepoll found that the biggest first-date faux pas a Brit can make is clicking your fingers at a waiter. Second was adding salt to the meal without tasting it first, while third was getting drunk. Other clangers in the top ten were licking the plate clean, burping, picking teeth with fingers, licking the knife, slurping soup, talking about sex or bodily functions and not leaving a tip.

Only 21% of the entire population of Wales can speak their native tongue.

The average bra size in Britain is 36C.

The most popular month to get married is August.

The most popular honeymoon destination for British couples is Thailand, followed by the Maldives, Dubai, Malaysia, Sri Lanka, the USA and Mauritius.

The population of Britain was just over 4 million in 1600. By 1901, it had increased to 40 million.

According to the Office for National Statistics, the proportion of people living alone in Britain has doubled since 1971, now accounting for 12% of the population.

A 2009 government survey found the karaoke machine to be the most irritating invention. The poll found that that nearly 25% of Brits wished it had never been invented. Other annoying creations included twenty-four-hour sports channels, computer games consoles, mobile phones and alarm clocks.

The oldest Mormon congregation in the world is in Preston, Lancashire.

One in three tickets sold at London theatres is for a musical.

The average person in the UK spends £16.08 on toilet rolls every year. The world average is just £2 per person.

Men will spend an average of £1,717,118 and women £1,363,729 during the course of a lifetime. Of that, £286,311 goes to the taxman.

The odds of winning the National Lottery jackpot are 13,983,816 to one, although the overall chance of getting a prize is fifty-four to one. A Camelot survey of winners found that the three most likely places for female winners to hide their tickets were in their bras, tights and knickers.

We send 3 billion emails in Britain every day, while the most popular time to use the Internet is between 5pm and 6pm on Sunday.

About 11% of the British population is left-handed.

Britain's oldest-ever person, Charlotte Hughes, was 115 years 228 days old when she died in 1993 at St David's Nursing home in Redcar, Cleveland. She had lived in her own home until 1991 when she began having trouble walking, and had put her longevity down to living 'a good honest life' and adherence to the Ten Commandments.

A great-grandmother discovered she had been celebrating her birthday on the wrong day for ninety-nine years. Elsie Aslett's error was only revealed when her family asked for her to receive a telegram from the Queen, and discovered she had been celebrating her birthday four days earlier her whole life after a pensions official spotted a discrepancy on her birth certificate.

One in ten people has a piercing other than on the earlobe.

Women are said to take an average of 89 seconds to use the loo, which is more than twice as long as the 39 seconds taken by the average man.

The average British person uses around 140 pints (80 litres) of water when having a bath.

A 2009 study of children between the ages of five and sixteen found they were spending an average of 2.7 hours per day watching television, 1.5 hours on the Internet and 1.3 hours on games consoles.

A total of 27% of British people have opened a bottle with their teeth.

Over 30% of British adults are single, with London home to the greatest number of unattached people – 51% of inner Londoners and 35% of suburban dwellers are not in a relationship.

In all, 23% of people admit to buying a new home to keep up with, or impress, their family and friends.

A 2008 survey found that women cause up to £20 million of damage to their possessions and themselves every year while exercising at home.

In December 2003, artist Mark McGowan attempted to sail from London to Glasgow in a supermarket trolley. He attached a sail to the trolley and used a broom for propulsion and steering. He hoped to complete the 400-mile (644-km) journey in nine months, but abandoned the voyage after just seventeen days due to bad weather.

The mean age of women giving birth in the UK is 29.2 years, while the average age of a first-time grandparent is 49.

Jim Webb from Sheffield lent £5 to a broke Australian to pay for a ferry trip in 1969. Traveller Gary Fenton promised to pay back the debt as soon as he could afford to and Webb passed on his address. When he heard no more, he thought nothing of it. However, in December 2008 Webb arrived home one day to discover Fenton, who was visiting England, had hand-delivered a card and £200 by way of repayment, nearly forty years later.

Spain is the top tourist destination for the Brits, with France, America, Greece and Italy next in line.

According to Relate, the three main reasons for couple's seeking their help in 2008 were affairs, dissatisfaction in the bedroom and work stress and lack of work–life balance.

Altogether, 53% of all homes in Great Britain have a Scrabble set. It is the best-selling board game in the country.

A recent study found that, while on the toilet, more than 14 million people in the UK read newspapers, books and magazines, 8 million people talk – either on the phone or to family – and one in five sends texts.

Around 18% of British men have had a vasectomy.

In 1998, the then Home Secretary, Jack Straw, revealed that MI5 held files on half a million people, but only 20,000 files were 'active' and of those, 13,000 were on British citizens.

The average person will own just three houses, 3 miles (4.8 km) apart, over the course of a lifetime.

An astonishing 69 members of the same family live in the same small street in Gateshead. The Hall family have come to dominate Cotswold Gardens since matriarch Catherine settled there in 1958. Mrs Hall had eight children, who went on to produce thirty-five grandchildren and nine great-grandchildren. Six of her children and their families now live in the street, along with three uncles and a mother-in-law. They occupy twelve of the houses.

The average midweek bedtime for people in Britain is between 10pm and 11pm.

In all, 10% of the British population suffer from some form of dyslexia.

Each Briton sends around sixty-seven text messages every month, more than three times the amount sent by the French and Germans. Meanwhile, mobile-phone use has doubled in the UK, from an average of five minutes a day to ten minutes, in just six years.

A total of 77% of Brits have lied about their child's age to get a reduced price for goods or tickets.

The average Brit spends 24 minutes on the Internet every day.

BONKERS BRITAIN

In December 2008, Powys Council accepted an offer from Mike Atherton, a resident of Llangynog, to pay £295 for the lights in his village to be lit until the end of March. They were turned off the previous September as part of a countywide drive to save money.

Arthur Reeder from Newport, Isle of Wight, has spent almost two decades collecting post boxes, and now has 190 in his garden. He became hooked on them in 1990 while out taking photographs of his first love, telephone boxes, in north Wales. He spotted a broken wooden post box lying in a skip outside the town's train station and bought it for just £20.

Meanwhile, David Morgan, from Burford in Oxfordshire, has a collection of 500 traffic cones. Morgan, who works for the world's largest producer of traffic cones, began his collection in 1986, while involved in a legal dispute with a rival manufacturer over the design of a cone. Mr Morgan scoured the country for cones to prove the design had existed previously. He won the case and carried on collecting.

Hannah Beswick was so scared of being buried alive that on her request, following her death in 1758, her body was embalmed and kept above ground, mounted inside a glass-fronted grandfather clock. It was stored in the house of her GP, Dr Charles White, who would check every day for signs of life. She was finally buried 110 years later.

The Ministry of Defence has amassed 160 files on UFOs, containing details of 8,000 sightings.

There were complaints of political correctness gone mad in 2006 when it was revealed that pre-school children attending two nurseries in Oxfordshire were being taught a new version of 'Baa Baa Black Sheep' – 'Baa Baa Rainbow Sheep'.

Under the heading 'Allergy Advice', plastic bottles of milk sold by the supermarket Asda are now carry the serious warning: 'Contains milk'.

On April Fool's Day 1980, the BBC reported that Big Ben was going to be converted so it gave a digital readout. This prompted a massive response from listeners protesting against the change. The BBC's Japanese service also announced that the clock hands would be sold to the first four listeners to contact them, leading one Japanese seaman in the mid-Atlantic to immediately radio in a bid.

In 2008, a massive £2 million was paid out to school pupils who successfully brought action against their local education authority, the majority of which were for accidents that would previously have been regarded as bad luck. These included Manchester City Council paying out £5,000 to a pupil who slipped on leaves in the playground; and £21,168 to a pupil in Rotherham who broke an ankle when playing 'tag'.

In September 1990, students at the Clarendon College of Further Education in Nottingham made a sherry trifle weighing 3.08 tons. It included 160 pints (91 litres) of sherry.

Farmer Giles Peare from West Sussex solved the problem of worms in his garden by eating them.

The World Gurning Championships are held at the Egremont Crab Fair in Cumbria every September, in a tradition dating back to 1266. Competitors pull faces through a horse's collar, the audience applauds and whoever receives the greatest applause wins.

A survey by The History Channel found that 21% of Brits believe the Pennines are to be found between France and Spain.

During the 18th century, it was believed that if a wealthy woman was naked when she married a man with debts, the creditors would not be able to reclaim their money from her.

The 19th-century geologist William Buckland, who gave us the first scientific description of what became known as the dinosaurs, owned a table made of fossilised poo, and used to ride around with a live bear on the back of his horse.

Twelve-year-old Donna Griffiths from Worcestershire began sneezing on 13 January 1981 and continued to sneeze for 978 days, sneezing once every minute at the beginning. This is the longest sneezing fit on record. By comparison, the average British person sneezes just four times a day.

In all, 8% of people store their underwear in the fridge in hot weather so they can keep cool.

In 1911, Brit Bobby Leach became the first person to go over the Niagara Falls in a steel barrel and survive.

The World Nettle Eating Championships takes place every year in the village of Marshwood, in Dorset. The event stems back to an argument in the pub in 1986 when two farmers were discussing who had the longest stinging nettles in their field. The longest-nettle competition eventually turned into the World Nettle Eating Championships when one of the farmers, Alex Williams, promised to eat any nettle that was longer than his.

British property developer Robert Blackwood applied for permission to be fed to Great White sharks off South Africa after he died, after watching a documentary on Gans Bay's sharks by the author of *Jaws*, Peter Benchley. A spokesperson for South Africa's Marine and Coastal Management Directorate said they could not grant the request because a state department was unable to commit to an event with an undetermined date.

British customs officials once seized an imported film entitled *Games In Bed*. When the film was eventually viewed by censors, they found it was about ways to entertain a sick child.

Golfer Reg Salisbury's ashes were blasted over his favourite course in a firework display. His family had his remains packed into thirty-six rockets for a £1,200 five-minute display at the Batchwoood course in St Albans, where Reg played every week.

Every September the World Black Pudding Throwing Championships take place at the Royal Oak pub in Ramsbottom, Bury. The contest, which is supposed to represent the Lancashire–Yorkshire rivalry, sees contestants from around the world trying to knock Yorkshire puddings off a 20-ft (6-m) ledge by throwing black puddings at them.

In 2009, a Lincoln couple who went to see a play billed as promising to make the audience 'laugh until they throw you out' were thrown out for laughing. Sharon Whitelaw and Tony Priestley were enjoying a performance of *Bouncers* at Lincoln's Drill Hall, but at the intermission they were told not to go back into the auditorium, as other theatregoers had complained about them.

Residents of a Nottinghamshire housing estate have installed pink lights, which show up teenagers' spots, in a bid to stop them gathering in the area.

The World's Biggest Liar competition is held every November at the Bridge Inn, Santon Bridge, in the Lake District. Politicians and lawyers are not allowed to enter.

GREAT BRITISH
CELEBRITIES

Before moving into television, *Who Wants to be a Millionaire?* presenter Chris Tarrant worked as a teacher and once lived for six months in his mini van in the school grounds. Tarrant's mail was delivered to his car, which had the registration 161 GLO. A friend once sent a letter addressed to 161 GLO, Sprules Road, London SE4, and the postman delivered it.

It took theatre impresario Sir Cameron Macintosh fifteen years to persuade Rowan Atkinson to play the part of Fagin in his stage production of *Oliver!* He only finally agreed after playing the part in his son's school play.

Hugh Grant was on the verge of quitting acting when he auditioned for *Four Weddings and a Funeral*. Aged thirty-two, he was fed up with not making the big time – and promised himself that unless he got the part he would stop trying.

Before finding fame, Denise van Outen, Billie Piper, Emma Bunton, Amy Winehouse, *I'm a Celebrity* winner Matt Willis and *EastEnders*' Samantha Janus all attended the Sylvia Young Theatre School.

Paul Merton, Anne Robinson, Sir Alan Sugar and Max Clifford, all failed the 11-plus.

Before becoming famous, television host Paul O'Grady worked in an abattoir, as a woodchopper and as a cleaner for singer Cleo Laine.

Sir Elton John insists the temperature of his dressing room must be 60 degrees Fahrenheit (15.6 degrees Celsius) in summer and 70 degrees Fahrenheit (21.1 degrees Celsius) in winter.

Rod Stewart, Des O'Connor, actor Michael Gambon, David Jason, news correspondent John Simpson and presenter Jonathan Dimbleby have all fathered children after the age of sixty.

Doctor Who star David Tennant was born David MacDonald, but had to change his surname on joining actor's union Equity, as there was already an actor of that name on the book. He chose Tennant, after reading an article about Pet Shop Boys singer Neil Tennant in *Smash Hits*.

Despite his strong American accent, *Doctor Who* and *Torchwood* star John Barrowman was actually born in Glasgow.

Many Americans mistakenly believe that Ricky Gervais wears bad false teeth for comedic purposes.

🐾 Bill Nighy's memorable character Davy Jones in *Pirates of the Caribbean: Dead Man's Chest* was computer animated, so instead of a heavy mask Bill only had to wear make-up round his eyes to blend in to the effects.

🐾 Singer Lily Allen is the daughter of *Robin Hood* actor Keith Allen.

🐾 British acting legend Sir John Gielgud is said to have had the longest-ever screen career. He made his film debut in 1924, when he appeared as the young lover of a married woman in *Who is the Man?*, with his last appearance coming 76 years later in the 2000 film *Catastrophe*.

🐾 Before finding fame, actress Amanda Holden and *GMTV* presenter Jenni Falconer both appeared as contestants on *Blind Date*.

🐾 The front covers of *Hello!* magazine's ten best-selling issues featured: Princess Diana's funeral (Sept 1997); Princess Diana's death (Sept 1997); Christmas issue featuring Madonna and Coronation Street (Dec 2000); the wedding of Prince Edward and Sophie Wessex (June 1999); the wedding of Paul and Sheryl Gascoigne (July 1996), Duchess of York 'My story' (Nov 1996); the wedding of Peter Phillips and Autumn Kelly (Nov 2008); the Princess Diana Story (Jan 1997); Elizabeth Taylor's wedding to Larry Fortensky(Oct 1991); and Princess Diana's dresses (Dec 1995).

🐾 Multi-millionaire and *Dragon's Den* dragon Duncan Bannatyne spent nine months in a military prison as a young man and received a dishonourable discharge for threatening to throw his commanding officer overboard.

John Cleese has a species of lemur named after him.

The manufacturers of an Eamonn Holmes-endorsed DVD game had to reprint 10,000 copies after his name was spelt incorrectly on the packaging. Holmes had noticed the error when he was sent a copy to sign.

Fashion guru Trinny Woodall was born Sarah-Jane, but became known by her nickname when, as a child, she was sent home from school for cutting off a fellow pupil's plait. Her father was friends with Ronald Searle, creator of the *St Trinian's* films, who remarked that she was just 'like a St Trinian's girl'.

Before wowing the world with his ice-skating prowess, Christopher Dean worked as a policeman. Skating partner Jayne Torvill was an insurance clerk.

Oscar-winning actor Sir Anthony Hopkins spent one week in the UK music charts in 1986 with the song 'Distant Star'. It reached number 75.

Weather presenter Siân Lloyd, singer Javine Hylton, model Nell McAndrew, Charlotte Church and Denise van Outen have all been named female Rear of the Year, while *Joseph* star Lee Mead, Will Young, Ronan Keating, Graham Norton, Robbie Williams and Frank Skinner have all been recipients of the male award.

Before earning Michelin stars as a cutting-edge chef, Heston Blumenthal worked as a debt collector.

Presenter and antiques expert David Dickinson gained the nickname 'The Duke' from a *Bargain Hunt* viewer who wrote in and suggested he looked a bit like John Wayne.

Stephen Merchant, creator and star of *The Office* and *Extras*, is 6 ft 7 inches (200 cm) tall.

Tony Benn, Shane MacGowan of The Pogues, singer Dido, Lord Andrew Lloyd Webber, writer Martin Amis and Sir John Gielgud all attended Westminster School.

In 1959, the pianist Liberace won £14,000 in damages from the *Daily Mirror* after the newspaper implied that he was gay. Liberace declared, 'I cried all the way to the bank!'

Radio 2 presenter Jeremy Vine is the brother of stand-up comedian and *Not Going Out* star Tim Vine.

Acting legend Peter O'Toole has been nominated eight times for the Academy Award for Best Actor in a Leading Role, making him the most-nominated actor never to win the award. His only Oscar has been an Honorary award, which was presented in 2007.

Noel Edmonds was once President of the Association of Gateaux Hurlers.

Time Team presenter Tony Robinson appeared as a stunt horse rider in *Carry On Cowboy*.

Jimmy Tarbuck owns the number plate COM 1C, while magician Paul Daniels owns MAG 1C.

Fern Britton's dad is Tony Britton, actor and star of 1980s sitcom *Don't Wait Up*.

Natasha Kaplinsky was once voted woman with the 'Most Ageing Hairstyle' in a women's magazine.

Stephen Fry spent several months in prison for credit-card fraud when he was eighteen. He was caught after a hotel receptionist in Swindon became suspicious of him, wondering why a boy who wore shabby shoes would be in possession of two credit cards.

Jonathan Ross was the first choice to present *TFI Friday*. Chris Evans went on to get the gig.

Comedian Frank Skinner was born Chris Collins, and took his stage name from a member of his local dominoes team.

Top Gear presenter Richard Hammond was driving at speeds of up to 288 mph (463 km/h) along an airfield near York, when the jet-powered car in which he was travelling crashed in September 2006.

BBC One Show presenter Adrian Chiles was once asked to join MI5; however, he failed the second interview.

Joan Collins's first husband, Maxwell Reed, tried to sell her to an Arab sheik for £10,000 only a few months after they married.

When Norman Wisdom was thirteen, he walked from London to Cardiff to get a job in the coal industry. It took him three weeks.

Trinidad-born newsreader Sir Trevor MacDonald learned to 'speak properly' by copying announcers he heard on the BBC's World Service.

When David Beckham first met the then Spice Girl Victoria Adams, he was so worried he would lose her phone number that he wrote it on half a dozen pieces of paper, which he placed in different places around the house.

Sir Lawrence Olivier is only the second actor to be buried in Poet's Corner in Westminster Abbey. The first was David Garrick.

Comedian Jimmy Carr was a Christian until his mid-twenties, and did not lose his virginity until he was twenty-six.

Chris Rea once wrote a song about Amanda Mealing, who plays Connie Beauchamp in *Holby City*.

Bruce Forsyth's catchphrases are so well known that some of them appear in *The Oxford Dictionary of Quotations*.

Graham Norton was once the victim of a knife attack during a mugging, He lost over half the blood in his body and one of his lungs collapsed.

The first people to win the Perrier Comedy Award were the Cambridge Footlights in 1981. The line-up included Stephen Fry, Hugh Laurie, Emma Thompson and Tony Slattery.

The 'E' in Richard E. Grant doesn't stand for anything.

David Jason was the third choice to play Del Boy in *Only Fools and Horses*. Actor Enn Reital was given the part initially, while the second choice was Oscar winner Jim Broadbent. When it came to start filming however, both had other work commitments, so were unable to take the part.

X Factor judge Louis Walsh managed his first band, Time Machine, at the age of fifteen.

Ron Moody only got the part of Fagin in Lionel Bart's 1968 musical adaptation of *Oliver!* after it had been turned down by Rex Harrison, Peter Sellers and Sid James.

Sex and the City star Kim Cattrall was actually born in Liverpool, and trained at the London Academy for Music and the Dramatic Arts.

A school teacher once wrote of *Gavin and Stacey* star James Corden, 'If he just gave the same level of commitment to work as to trying to make other people laugh, he would be a grade-A student.'

Television antiques expert David Dickinson has had the same haircut since 1969.

British actor Kenneth Williams had an obsession about toilets. He constantly suffered from piles and would not use other people's toilets. At theatres he always insisted on his own personal toilet paper and any visitors to his home had to use the toilet at Tottenham Court Road Tube station.

Vanessa Redgrave is the only person in Oscar history to win a Best Supporting Actress gong for playing the title role in a film. The film was *Julia*.

Bond star Roger Moore's first wife, Doorn van Steyn, advised him to get out of acting because he had no chance of getting anywhere in the profession. She said that his face was too weak, his chin too big and his mouth too small.

Gary Oldman's sister is Laila Morse, who plays Mo Harris in *EastEnders*.

British film star Vivien Leigh auditioned for the role of Scarlett O'Hara in *Gone with the Wind* after filming of the epic had begun.

Sean Connery wore a toupee in all his Bond films.

Des O'Connor had rickets as a child and spent several years in callipers, only walking properly when he was six or seven.

In 1998, Welsh soprano Katherine Jenkins shattered a crystal chandelier at Swansea's Brangwyn Hall while singing 'Oh Holy Night'.

Have I Got News For You's Paul Merton was born Paul Martin, but re-named himself after the region of south London where he grew up.

Ghandi star Ben Kingsley was born Krishna Bhanji.

Oscar winner Dame Helen Mirren is another famous thespian who changed her name. She was born Ilyena Vasilievna Mironov.

Harry Potter star Daniel Radcliffe revealed that Australian fans think he is *Lord of the Rings* hero Elijah Wood.

Rupert Grint had never done any professional acting before he won the role of Ron Weasley in the Harry Potter films.

As a child, Catherine Zeta Jones suffered from a viral infection that impaired her breathing and led to her having a tracheotomy – the scar is still visible today.

Nigel Havers once worked as a researcher on Radio 2's *Jimmy Young Show*.

Pirates of the Caribbean star Orlando Bloom was named after the 17th-century composer Orlando Gibbons.

While at school at Clifton College in Bristol, John Cleese painted footsteps to suggest that the school's statue of Field Marshal Haig had left his plinth to walk to the toilet to relieve himself.

Only Fools and Horses star David Jason was twenty-six before he got into acting. Prior to that, he worked as an electrician.

Joan Collins was separated from her first husband by the age of twenty-one.

Dame Judi Dench's Oscar-winning performance as Queen Elizabeth I in *Shakespeare in Love* lasted just eight minutes.

Jonathan Creek star Alan Davies once considered adopting the stage name Rochester Snodland. He's also performed as Alan Balgonie.

Strictly Come Dancing legend and political reporter John Sergeant was vice captain of his school rugby team. His captain was DJ Tony Blackburn.

James Bond star Daniel Craig is the first Bond actor to have been born after the Bond series began. He is also the shortest actor to play the role of James Bond, despite standing 5 ft 11 inches (180 cm).

After signing up to play 007, Craig started checking into hotels under the name Jimmy Bond.

One time 'It-girl' and sometime television presenter Tara Palmer-Tomkinson is a trained concert pianist.

Sir Richard Attenborough used 300,000 extras for the funeral scene in *Gandhi*. Eleven camera crews shot 20,000 ft (6,096 m) of film for the scene, longer than the whole film that was finally released, yet only 125 seconds was ever used.

Attenborough says the reason he calls everyone 'darling' and 'luvvie' is nothing to do with loving them. He is just appalling at remembering names.

Mamma Mia! star Julie Walters originally trained to be a nurse.

When Walters was born, her umbilical cord was wrapped round her neck. She was not expected to survive and a priest was called to read the last rites to her and her mother.

Chef Gordon Ramsay has size-15 feet, and has to have all his shoes specially made for him.

EastEnders star Barbara Windsor has size-1 feet.

British star Ralph Fiennes is the only actor ever to win a Tony Award for playing *Hamlet* on Broadway.

Fern Britton's sister is married to children's television legend Brian Cant.

Vivien Leigh was a heavy smoker, getting through almost four packs a day during filming of *Gone With The Wind*.

Before becoming a comedian, Jimmy Carr worked in the marketing department of Shell Oil.

Kate Winslet was nicknamed Blubber as a teenager because of her weight.

Winslet, J.K. Rowling and Sarah Ferguson were all head girls at their schools.

Most famous for his role as the bald-headed captain of the Starship Enterprise, Patrick Stewart began losing his hair when he was just nineteen.

Before finding fame in *Marion and Geoff* and *Gavin and Stacey*, Rob Brydon worked as a presenter on a shopping channel.

Michael Gambon auditioned for the role of James Bond after George Lazenby. But he was turned down because the producers didn't want another unknown actor – which Gambon was at the time – playing 007.

When she was eight, Carol Vorderman's teacher wrote in her school report that 'Carol has a masterly hold over mathematical computation which should prove profitable later on'.

Although *Strictly Come Dancing* star Brendan Cole has been dancing since he was six, it was not his first career. He is one of the few professional dancers to have previously worked as a builder.

Bruce Forsyth was evacuated from London at the start of World War II, but returned after just three days as he was so homesick.

Forsyth was going to call himself Jack Johnson when he started out in show business. However there was already a heavyweight boxer of the same name, so he decided to keep his own name instead.

A survey found that six out of ten people do not know which is Ant and which is Dec. For reference, Ant always stands on the left-hand side of your television screen.

TV chef Rick Stein first moved to Padstow, Cornwall, in 1975 to open a nightclub. It was only when the club failed that Rick turned to the restaurant business instead.

Kate Winslet's first acting job was dancing with the Honey Monster in an advert for Sugar Puffs cereal.

Barbara Windsor appeared in just nine of the thirty *Carry On* films made.

GREAT BRITISH INVENTORS AND INVENTIONS

🐶 A Post Office engineer testified before Government that the telephone, then in its infancy, would prove to be of little use because most messages were already carried by errand boys or messengers.

🐶 Peter Chilvers was just twelve years old when he came up with the idea for a rudder-steered board powered by a sail in 1958, while on Hayling Island. It was to become known as windsurfing.

🐶 James Snell of London created the first chair that was designed specifically for dental work in 1832. Snell's chair featured both a back and a seat that allowed for minor adjustment. Before this time, if you went to a dentist with a toothache and the removal of your tooth was prescribed, your dentist may have asked you to sit on the floor, at which point he would have stood behind you and secured your head between his knees. This position was ideal for two reasons: it provided easy access to your teeth and it kept your head still.

Sir Clive Sinclair, inventor of the Spectrum computer, doesn't use the Internet.

Sir Isaac Newton is believed to have invented the first cat flap. While Newton was in his attic trying to conduct light experiments, his cat kept nudging the door open and letting the light in, spoiling his experiments. So Newton decided to cut a small opening in the doorway, which he then covered with felt, attached to the top of the opening.

Sir Isaac Newton once wrote in a letter that the date of Armageddon would be 2060.

The piers in Brighton West, Margate, Blackpool North, Aberystwyth, Deal, Hornsea, Lytham, Plymouth, New Brighton, Eastbourne, Scarborough, Weston-super-Mare Birnbeck, Hastings and Bournemouth were all designed and engineered by the same man: Eugenius Birch.

Not content with just building piers, Birch also designed and built the West Surrey waterworks, the Devon and Somerset railway, Exmouth docks and Ilfracombe harbour.

John Jaques, a well-known London maker and publisher of games, introduced the game of Snap in 1866, using illustrations of the characters he had used in his previous Happy Families game.

Alexander Graham Bell never used his telephone to call his wife or mother, as they both suffered from deafness.

Sir Hiram Stevens Maxim, inventor of the first portable machine gun, also invented the mousetrap.

In 1784, Joseph Bramah patented the Bramah safety lock, which for many years had the reputation of being unpickable. He offered £200 to anyone who could pick his lock. Although many tried it, it was not until 1851 that the money was won by an American, A.C. Hobbs – although it took him sixteen days to do it.

During the late 19th century, 43 patents were filed for moustache guards that stopped food getting stuck in a man's moustache while he was eating.

Nottingham Forest were the first football team to wear shin guards, which were invented by club player Samuel Widdowson in 1874. At the time, the hacking of shins, tripping up, and elbowing were allowed, and the goalkeeper could be charged out of the way of a shot even if he was nowhere near the ball.

Queen Anne granted Henry Mill the first patent for a typewriter in 1714. It was never made however, and the first typewriter did not appear for almost another century.

The idea of British Summer Time was first proposed by keen horse-rider William Willett, who was infuriated by the 'waste' of useful daylight first thing in the morning, during summer. He couldn't believe that although the sun had been up for hours during his rides through his local woods, people were still asleep in bed. He made his first proposal in 1907 and died still fighting for it in 1915. It was introduced in 1916.

James Dyson built 5,127 prototypes while developing his vacuum cleaner.

The vacuum cleaner was not invented by Hoover, but by British bridge engineer Hubert Cecil Booth, who took out a patent on his 'suction cleaning device' in 1901. The motor and pump were so big that they remained on a horse-drawn carriage outside along with the vacuum cleaner, while hoses of more than 200 m (656 ft) were taken into the house that was to be cleaned. Booth later introduced transparent hoses, so people could watch the dirt being sucked out of their homes.

The first multi-purpose food processor was invented in 1950 by Ken Wood.

When John Logie Baird, inventor of the television, was just 13, he demonstrated signs of his ingenuity by rigging up a telephone exchange to connect his bedroom to those of his friends across the street, using two biscuit tins and some thread.

John Wilkinson, the 18th-century inventor of the first-ever iron ship, was buried in an iron coffin.

Although the American Wright brothers were the first people to execute a controlled flight in a plane, wealthy British aristocrat Sir George Cayley is described by aviation experts as the father of aeronautics. He designed his first aircraft as long ago as 1799, and by the middle of the 19th century he was building and flying gliders.

Prior to Thomas Allbutt's invention of the clinical thermometer in 1866, patients were required to hold a 1-ft-long (30-cm) thermometer in their hands. Using this method, it took about twenty minutes for an acceptable measurement of body temperature to be provided.

The policeman's whistle was invented by Birmingham toolmaker Thomas Hudson in 1883. It came in response to an advert from the Metropolitan Police, who were looking for a more effective replacement for the rattle, which was then in use for communication. Hudson's police whistle could be used hands-free and the sound carried for over a mile. The first order from the police was for 21,000.

Trevor Baylis, inventor of the clockwork radio, once performed with the Berlin State Circus and also worked as an underwater stuntman.

The first electric toaster was produced by Crompton and Company in 1893. Unfortunately, it could only toast one side of the bread at a time. Moreover, electric power was not yet widely available, and then often only at night, as households used electricity almost exclusively for lighting. Consequently, the toaster was not a success.

After deciding that drinks marquees were boring and lacking atmosphere, British designer Andi Francis spent nine months designing a travelling tavern. The inflatable building he created holds up to thirty people at a time and comes complete with blow-up bar, fireplace, a stuffed fish mounted on one wall and mock-Tudor beams.

The friction match was invented by accident by chemist John Walker in 1826. He had been mixing potassium chloride, antimony sulphide, gum and starch at the time, when he scraped his mixture stick across some stones to clean it, and it burst into flames. He never bothered to patent his invention, preferring to pursue his scientific studies. It was a certain Samuel Jones from London who saw Walker's matches and decided to market them, calling his matches 'Lucifer's'. They became popular, especially among smokers, although they did have a bad burning smell.

Frank Whittle filed the first patent for a jet engine in 1930, although it was not built until 1937 and did not fly until 1941.

A small fixing problem in the British Museum is said to have led to the invention of the Rawlplug. The Museum needed electrical fittings fixed to walls unobtrusively and without causing damage to the masonry. This was difficult using the traditional method – chiselling a hole in the masonry, plugging it with wood, and screwing the fitting to the wood. John J. Rawlings, a building contractor, solved the problem by inventing the fibre plug into which screws were driven.

The first rubber band was made in 1845 by Stephen Perry of the rubber manufacturing company Messers Perry and Co. in London. Perry invented the band, which was made of vulcanised rubber, to hold papers or envelopes together.

The fax machine was invented in the 19th century. It was devised and patented by Scottish clock maker Alexander Bain in 1843, and actually pre-dates the telephone.

Alexander Graham Bell, inventor of the telephone, beat rival inventor Elisha Gray to the patent office by just two hours on 7 March 1876.

Between the years AD 1000 and 1010, a monk from Malmesbury Abbey named Elmer built the world's first glider. He flew 200 yd (183 m) before crashing and breaking his legs.

John Dunlop's great invention, the pneumatic tyre, came about by chance. In 1888, his small son was prescribed cycling as cure for a heavy cold, so Dunlop hit on the idea of making the boy's tricycle more comfortable by fitting it with inflated tubes, made of canvas and bonded together with liquid rubber. He patented this idea, using the word 'pneumatic' for the first time.

Rubber got its name in 1770, when chemist Joseph Priestley discovered that the material would rub out pencil.

London office worker Mercedes Gleitz proved the reliability of the world's first waterproof watch by wearing one on his wrist while he swam the English Channel in 1927.

The knitting machine was invented in 1589 by the clergyman William Lee, who was tormented by the constant clack-clacking of his wife's knitting needles. He imagined a device that, instead of producing one loop at a time, could knit an entire row of loops at once. When he asked Queen Elizabeth I to patent the device she refused, so Lee left England to try his luck at the court of King Henri IV of France. Although the French sovereign granted Lee the privileges he sought, before the inventor could establish himself Henri IV was assassinated. Lee died penniless, although his invention went on to become a massive success and was used right up until the 19th century.

Robert Yeates invented the can-opener in 1855, forty-five years after British merchant Peter Durand transformed food preservation with his 1810 patenting of the tin can. Until then, people used a hammer and chisel to open cans.

The inventor of the lava lamp, Craven Walker, also produced *Travelling Light*, the first naturist film to go on general release in Britain.

The first message sent by Samuel Morse in January 1838, using his Morse code, read 'A patient waiter is no loser'.

The first person to set up a mail-order business was Pryce Pryce-Jones of Newtown in Wales, who began selling local Welsh flannels this way during the 1870s. People would choose what they wanted from leaflets he sent out and the goods would then be dispatched by post and train. By 1880, he had more than 100,000 customers.

Thomas Crapper, a British plumber, developed a type of flushing toilet in 1872. He perfected the cistern – the tank that holds the water for flushing and made flushing quieter. American soldiers stationed in England during World War I used his name as a euphemism for the toilet, a habit that they took with them when they returned to the USA.

When inventor of the computer Charles Babbage was eight years old, he was sent to a country school to recover from a life-threatening fever. His parents ordered that his 'brain was not to be taxed too much'.

Frank Hornby, who patented Meccano, was originally going to call it 'Mechanics Made Easy'.

British metallurgist Harry Brearley invented stainless steel by accident, while attempting to develop a steel that would resist the heat inside a gun.

Before becoming known as the inventor of the miner's safety lamp, Sir Humphrey Davy worked on gases, particularly nitrous oxide, otherwise known as laughing gas. As well as suggesting it might prove useful during operations, he also used it during his parties, to ensure his guests would all have a good laugh.

Ron Hickman invented the Black & Decker Workmate workbench in 1961 after a home DIY disaster. He had sawn a chair in half while struggling to hold the item and saw it at the same time and so decided to make an extra hand to help with his DIY. Hickman's idea was rejected by manufacturers for many years, and led to him selling it himself mail order, before Black & Decker started production over a decade later. Hickman was also responsible for the design of the original Lotus Elan.

GREAT BRITISH ROYALTY

🐾 Queen Elizabeth I used to appear in public with fine cloth stuffed in her mouth, as the loss of her front teeth had caused her face to sink inwards.

🐾 William the Conqueror ordered that everyone should go to bed at 8 o'clock.

🐾 In 2002, at 76 years of age, Queen Elizabeth II became the oldest monarch to celebrate a Golden Jubilee. The youngest was James I (James VI of Scotland) at fifty-one years old.

🐾 It is believed that Anne Boleyn suffered from polydactyly – she had six fingers on her left hand.

🐾 King George III was such a fan of farming, he would write to agriculture journals using the alias Ralph Robinson.

🐾 King Charles I wore two shirts to his execution as it was a cold day and he thought if he shivered people would think him a coward.

🐑 In 2009, Henry VIII's last suit of armour was put on display at the Royal Armouries in Leeds to mark 500 years since he took the throne. The waist measurement was a whopping 52 inches (132 cm).

🐑 Queen Victoria banned the colour black from her funeral – traditional black mourning hangings were banished from London's streets and replaced with purple cashmere and white satin bows.

🐑 Victoria outlived three of her nine children and eleven of her 42 grandchildren.

🐑 Richard II died in 1400 and was buried in Westminster Abbey – however, his jawbone was stolen by a schoolboy in 1776. It was finally returned by the boy's descendants in 1906.

🐑 King Henry VIII was a spoiled child who had his own whipping boy. The boy was punished every time the young prince did something wrong.

🐑 The British monarch who had the most children was Edward I. He had sixteen offspring – six sons and ten daughters.

🐑 The cruise liner *The Queen Mary* was originally to have had a different name. A director of Cunard, the ship's owners, met King George V intending to name the ship 'Queen Victoria'. He asked if the vessel could be named after 'the greatest queen this country has ever known'. The King replied, 'That is the greatest compliment ever paid to my wife. I'll ask her.' Hence, the ship became the Queen Mary.

Queen Elizabeth II is the second longest-reigning monarch in the world. Only Bhumibol Adulyadej of Thailand has reigned longer, having ascended to the throne in June 1946, almost six years before Elizabeth.

Queen Victoria was just eighteen years old when she ascended the throne.

Since 1066 there have been five Queen Elizabeths – Edward IV's wife, Henry VII's wife, Queen Elizabeth I, George VI's wife and Queen Elizabeth II.

The largest king's ransom in history was raised in 1194 by Richard the Lionheart, to buy his release from Holy Roman Emperor Henry VI. The English people were forced to contribute almost 150,000 marks to free their king, who didn't actually speak a word of English.

The last British king to be born abroad was King George II, who was born in Hanover in Germany on 10 November 1683.

Prince Frederick, eldest son of George II, failed to become king. He died after being hit on the head by a cricket ball. Known as 'Poor Fred', he was hated by his family, who all refused to attend his funeral.

The Prince of Wales's recovery from typhoid in 1871 was widely thought to have resulted from nationwide prayers, not from advances in medicine.

Henry V created the world's first passports. They were designed to help prove who you were if you travelled to a foreign land.

Because of Prince Edward's size at birth – he weighed only 5lb 11oz (2.6 kg) – the Queen had expected him to be a girl, and had chosen only female names.

At the age of fourteen, Prince William was one of the top 100 fastest swimmers in the country.

Prince Charles is paid one daffodil every year by the Isles of Scilly Wildlife Trust as rent for all the empty land, islands and rocks within the isles.

King Edward VIII was the first member of the Royal Family to act in a movie, appearing in three silent films during 1919. Prince Charles was the first member to speak on screen in a fictional movie, appearing opposite John Cleese in Video Arts' environmental film *Grimes Goes Green* in 1990.

Queen Elizabeth II has been portrayed 22 times on film.

In 1858, Queen Victoria's toilet was decorated in gold.

The first recorded use of fireworks in Britain was at the wedding of King Henry VII to Elizabeth of York in 1486.

For 116 years, between 1714 and 1830, there was always a King George on the throne: George I (1714–1727), George II (1727–1760), George III (1760–1820) and George IV (1820–1830).

Queen Victoria's lady-in-waiting, Anna Russell, the Duchess of Bedford, inadvertently created what is now known as afternoon tea during the mid-19th century. With English dinners typically at 7pm, she often found herself feeling faint as the day wore on, so she started sipping tea each afternoon to tide her over and had her servants bring her a few little bites of food to eat as she sipped her tea. This soon became a daily ritual that the Duchess and her friends indulged in every afternoon.

Princess Anne was not required to take a sex test when she competed in the 1976 Olympic Games.

Among the many appointments made by the Royal Household are Keeper of the Royal Philatelic Collection, Royal Goat Herd, Royal Swan Keeper, Surveyor of the Queen's Pictures and Royal Herb Strewer.

The last coronation of an English monarch not to take place at Westminster Abbey was that of Edward the Confessor in 1042, who was crowned at Winchester. It was he, a few years later, who established an abbey known as West Minster, on a marshy island in the Thames.

Diana, Princess of Wales, was the seventh cousin of Humphrey Bogart.

Queen Elizabeth II has a Gold Blue Peter badge.

King Henry VIII could wear out up to eight horses a day while hunting.

Each successive monarch faces in a different direction on British coins.

The Royal Family costs the equivalent of 66p per person per year in the UK.

Sculptor Arnold Machin was responsible for the famous effigy of Queen Elizabeth II that appears on UK postage stamps. The 1966 design is said to be so well liked by the Queen that she has declined to have it updated and changed over the years, unlike her effigy on coinage. More than 320 billion copies have been made over the last forty years, making it the most reproduced work of art in history.

Queen Elizabeth I suffered from anthophobia – a fear of roses.

King Richard II is credited with inventing the handkerchief, more than 600 years ago.

In 2008, a lorry carrying 2,000 pints (1,137 litres) of lager destined for a pub called the Windsor Castle was delivered to the Queen's residence by mistake.

In 1066, 1483 and 1936 there were three kings on the British throne during the course of the year. Edward the Confessor, King Harold and William the Conqueror in 1066; Edward IV, Edward V and Richard III in 1483; and George V, Edward VIII and George VI in 1936.

Viscount Linley was the first member of the Royal Family to sue a newspaper. He won damages against *Today* in 1990.

Prince Charles took his seat in the House of Lords in 1969, when he was twenty-one, but could have sat in Parliament from the age of three-and-a-half. Only the Dukes of Cornwall – always the eldest son of the monarch – have this right to sit at any age.

Prince Charles owns a collection of toilet seats.

When the British film *The Madness of King George III* was released in America, the 'III' was dropped. This was because it was thought that American filmgoers would believe it to be a sequel, and not go see it because they had never seen *The Madness of King George I* and *II*.

In 1558, Queen Elizabeth I introduced a tax on beards because she didn't like them.

King Henry III suffered from ailurophobia, an irrational fear of cats. Ailurophobics are particularly afraid of cats staring at them and can faint if this goes on for too long.

Twenty-three wedding cakes were made for the nuptials of Prince Charles and Lady Diana Spencer.

In 1864, Queen Victoria's husband, Prince Albert, helped put out a fire in the nursery of Marlborough House, the home of the Prince and Princess of Wales. He enjoyed the experience so much that he asked the fire brigade if he could help fight other fires in the capital. They said yes, and a year later he was present when a blaze destroyed the 17th-century Saville House in Leicester Square. Victoria was not amused.

King Harold, King William II and King Richard I were all killed by arrows.

King Henry VI of England became King when he was just eight months old.

King George VI is the only member of the British Royal Family to have ever competed at Wimbledon. He entered the doubles event in 1926 with his Royal Air Force tennis partner, Wing Commander Louis Grieg. They lost in the opening round.

When the Queen leaves Buckingham Palace to attend the State Opening of Parliament every year, an MP is ceremonially 'held hostage' at the Palace to ensure that the monarch isn't kidnapped or executed by any treasonous MPs.

The Coronation Oil, which is used to anoint the new sovereign seated in the Coronation Chair in Westminster Abbey, is a secret formula but is said to include oils of orange flowers, roses, cinnamon, jasmine, musk and ambergris.

King Richard III was born with teeth.

King Alexander III of Scotland died when his horse jumped over a cliff while they were out riding at night.

Henry VIII, Charles I, George V and George VI were all second sons who became King.

The Queen no longer sends telegrams to people on their 100th birthday – she sends cards.

All of Henry VIII's wives were related to each other.

King Henry VIII declared his marriage to Anne of Cleves void after just six months because he thought she was ugly. Henry was also reported to have been enjoying a game of tennis while his wife Anne Boleyn was being beheaded.

Kings William I, William II, Stephen, Henry II, Richard II and Edward IV were all born in France.

Lady Elizabeth Bowes-Lyon, later to be known as the Queen Mother, turned down the proposal of the then Prince Albert four times before accepting him.

Sgt Charles Burley Ward was the last man to receive the Victoria Cross from Queen Victoria herself. He was awarded the VC for bravery in the Boer War.

King Henry VIII's last wife, Catherine Parr, is England's most married queen. She tied the knot four times. Her final husband, Thomas Seymour, was the brother of Jane Seymour – Henry's VIII's third wife.

Queen Eleanor, wife of Edward I, was so upset on seeing her husband critically ill, after poison had set into a battle wound, that she personally sucked all of the poison out of the wound herself. He survived, but she died as a result.

In July 2003, Madame Tussauds' Wax Museum eliminated immediate members of the British Royal Family from its royal exhibit for the first time in 200 years. Prince Andrew was one of those eliminated.

Queen Victoria was the first person to appear on a British postage stamp – the Penny Black.

King Charles I had a lucky black cat. However, the very day after the cat died, Charles was arrested and was subsequently beheaded.

By the end of his life, King Henry VIII's waistline is said to have measured 4.5 ft (1.37 m) round.

The first king to wear a crown for his coronation was Edward the Elder, King of the West Saxons, who ruled from AD 899 to 924.

Buckingham Palace has 775 rooms. These include 19 state rooms, 52 royal and guest bedrooms, 188 staff bedrooms, 92 offices and 78 bathrooms.

King Charles II was the last king to be crowned twice – the first time at Scone in Scotland on 1 January 1651, and the second a formal coronation ten years later at Westminster Abbey on 23 April 1661.

Princess Anne was the first daughter of a sovereign to attend boarding school.

In 1938, Queen Elizabeth II – then Princess Elizabeth – was given the world's smallest watch as a gift from the people of France. She wore it all the time, even to her wedding and coronation; however, she lost it in 1955. In 1957 when she made a State visit to France, she was presented with a replacement watch that was nearly as small.

King Henry V was only sixteen years old when he took part in the Battle of Shrewsbury.

The site where Buckingham Palace now stands was originally a mulberry garden planted by King James I (reigned 1603–25) to rear silkworms. Unfortunately, he chose the wrong kind of mulberry bush, and silk production never took off in Britain.

Prince Philip was reportedly born on a dining-room table.

Although King Richard I ruled for ten years, he only spent six months of his reign in England.

Mary Queen of Scots became a widow at the age of just eighteen when her husband, King Francis II of France, died.

Queen Elizabeth I owned 2,000 gowns, which were kept in a separate clothing house.

The Queen does not have or need a passport. She also does not need a driver's licence.

King Edward VIII is the only monarch to have published an autobiography.

Princess Anne was the target of a failed kidnap attempt in March 1974 when Ian Ball, a 26-year-old man with mental health problems, ambushed her car in the Mall, London. He had asked her to 'Come with me for a day or two' because he wanted £2 million. The Princess was said to have replied, 'Not bloody likely, and I haven't got £2 million!'

The Queen sent her first email in 1976 from an Army base.

Edward VII used to weigh his guests after weekends at Sandringham to ensure that they had eaten well.

When Prince Charles was born his father, the Duke of Edinburgh, described him as a 'plum pudding' and for a time the name stuck with the media.

King George V kept all 180 of the clocks at Sandringham 30 minutes fast, so that he would never be late for an appointment.

King George IV got so drunk on the day of his wedding to Caroline of Brunswick that he had to be carried to the altar.

When Prince Andrew was born in 1960, he was the first baby born to a reigning monarch since 1857.

The Queen's racing colours are a purple body with gold braid, scarlet sleeves and black velvet cap with gold fringe.

The Queen is the only person in Britain legally allowed to eat swan.

Queen Victoria used to use marijuana to ease premenstrual cramps.

All of Queen Anne's seventeen children died before her.

Towards the end of her reign, Queen Victoria became weak and worried about dropping her grandchildren during the sittings for family photographs. A maid was brought in to sit underneath the Queen's vast dress to hold the babies securely in place.

George IV used to clip a lock of hair from each woman that he slept with and kept them in individual envelopes, bearing the owner's name. When he died, more than 7,000 envelopes were found in his bedroom.

Elizabeth I used a portable toilet shaped like a box covered with red velvet and trimmed in lace with a lid and carrying handles.

Legend has it that Sir Walter Raleigh once bet Queen Elizabeth I that he could measure the weight of smoke. To win the bet, Raleigh placed a piece of tobacco on one end of a balancing scale. He then filled his pipe with an equal amount, smoked it, and carefully tapped the ash onto the other end of the scale. The difference in weight, he said, was the weight of the smoke. Elizabeth paid Raleigh his winnings, declaring that she had seen many men turn their gold to smoke, but she had never before seen smoke turned into gold.

King George I of England could not speak English. He was born and raised in Germany and never learned to speak English, even though he was King from 1714 to 1727. He left the running of the country to his ministers.

Prince Philip is the Queen's second cousin. Both are great-grandchildren of Queen Victoria. Philip's parents, Prince Andrew of Greece and Princess Alice of Battenberg, fled to France with their five young children to avoid the Prince's almost certain execution.

Prince Harry has two private secretaries to deal with his love letters from fans.

GREAT BRITISH WEATHER

In April 1884, an earthquake in East Anglia killed four people.

In terms of average annual temperature, the warmest place in the UK is the Scilly Isles, with a mean temperature of 11.5 degrees Celsius (52.7 degrees Fahrenheit).

St Helier in Jersey is the sunniest town in the British Isles, with an average of 1,915 hours of sunshine every year. This compares with many coastal resorts along the south coast of England that have 1,750 hours of sunshine per year.

Meanwhile, Braemar in Aberdeenshire is the coldest low-level place in the UK, with a mean temperature of just 6.5 degrees Celsius (43.7 degrees Fahrenheit).

On Sunday, 6 August 2000, a shower of dead sprats fell on Great Yarmouth in Norfolk. A mini-tornado had swept up the tiny silver fish from the North Sea and carried them for 2 miles (3.2 km) before depositing them on the seaside resort.

In 1918, during a torrential rainstorm, several hundred dead sand eels fell from the sky over the Hendon district of Sunderland.

There are about 200 earthquakes a year in Britain.

The average English rain shower lasts two-and-a-half hours. It is most likely to be raining at 7am and least likely at 3am.

In 1815, Mount Tambora in Indonesia erupted, killing 92,000 people. As the global climate effects of the volcanic eruption became apparent, 1816 became known as the 'year without a summer'. Aerosols from Tambora blocked out sunlight and reduced global temperatures by 3 degrees Celsius (37.4 degrees Fahrenheit). Europe missed a summer and crops across Britain failed. Things were so bad that the Government suspended taxes for the year.

The year 2006 was the warmest on record for the whole of the country. The average temperature was 9.7 degrees Celsius (49.5 degrees Fahrenheit), 1.1 degree higher than the long-term average.

The highest-ever recorded temperature in Britain is 38.5 degrees Celsius (101.3 degrees Fahrenheit) at Brogdale, Faversham in Kent on 10 August 2003. The coldest recorded temperature is an incredible -27.2 degrees Celsius (-17 degrees Fahrenheit) at Braemar, Aberdeenshire, on 11 February 1895 and again on 10 January 1982.

For fourteen days at Heathrow Airport between 23 June and 8 July 1976, the temperature was above 31 degrees Celsius (87.8 degrees Fahrenheit).

The heaviest rainfall in the UK was recorded at Sprinking Tarn in Cumbria in 1954, when 6,528 mm (257 in) fell in one year.

The longest drought ever experienced in the UK occurred in Sussex, and lasted sixty days between 17 March and 15 May 1893.

In terms of annual average rainfall, the driest recorded place in the UK is St Osyth, Essex, which has just 513 mm (20 in) per year.

The coldest recorded year in the UK was 1740, with an average temperature of just 6.86 degrees Celsius (44.35 degrees Fahrenheit).

Crib Goch in Snowdonia, Wales, is said to be the wettest place in the UK with an average annual rainfall of 4,472.3 mm (176.1 in).

In Martinstown, near Dorchester in Dorset, 279 mm (11 in) of rain fell in only twenty-four hours on 18 July 1955...

... while on 10 August 1893, 32 mm (1.3 in) of rain fell in Preston, Lancashire, in just five minutes.

The Dogger Bank earthquake in 1931 was the strongest ever recorded in the UK. It measured 6.1 on the Richter scale. The tremor began at around 1:30am on 7 June 1931 on Dogger Bank, 60 miles (96.5 km) off the Yorkshire coast in the North Sea. The effects were felt throughout the country: a church spire in Filey became twisted, chimneys fell throughout East Yorkshire and a head fell off a waxwork in Madame Tussauds in London.

Two million homes have been built in the natural floodplain of rivers or the coast and are vulnerable to flooding.

Weather records for the UK date back to 26 August 55 BC.

The highest-ever gust of wind at a high-level site came on 20 March 1986, when a burst of 150 knots (173 mph; 277.8 km/h) was recorded at the Cairngorm Automatic Weather Station.

The earliest snow in London fell on 25 September 1885.

The snowiest winter of the 20th century in the UK was 1947. Snow fell in some part of the country every day between 22 January and 17 March.

Snowflakes can take as long as one hour to fall to the ground.

In 1954, George Cowling became the first television weatherman.

The worst avalanche ever to take place in this country occurred in Lewes, East Sussex, on 27 December 1836. Eight people were killed and several houses were destroyed.

December is usually the wettest month of the year.

The temperature by rivers and canals located close to city centres is up to 5 degrees cooler than the temperature in town and city centres.

You are actually more likely to be struck by lightning than scoop the jackpot in the National Lottery.

In England and Wales, there is a 2% increase in mortality for every degree below 19 degrees Celsius (66.2 degrees Fahrenheit). Around half of these deaths are caused by respiratory conditions and half by strokes and heart attacks.

Although the wettest parts of Britain have around ten times as much rain as the driest parts of the country, there is much less difference in the number of rain days. The driest parts have between 150 and 200 rain days per year, while the wettest parts have just over 200 rain days.

You are most likely to hear thunder if you live in East Anglia, the east Midlands and the south-east of England.

The heavy rain of summer 2007 led to 55,000 homes and businesses in Britain becoming flooded. About half the 630 miles (1,014 km) of flood defences tested by the floods were overwhelmed. Rivers were at their highest levels for sixty years during the wettest May to July for 250 years.

The Met Office was formed in 1854, with the aim of helping sailors know what was happening with the weather.

Since 2002, the sea areas used in the shipping forecast are: Viking, North Utsire, South Utsire, Forties, Cromarty, Forth, Tyne, Dogger, Fisher, German Bight, Humber, Thames, Dover, Wight, Portland, Biscay, Trafalgar, FitzRoy, Sole, Lundy, Fastnet, Irish Sea, Shannon, Rockall, Malin, Hebrides, Bailey, Fair Isle, Faeroes and South-east Iceland.

There were 900 heat-related deaths in Great Britain during the European summer heat wave of 2003, which is said to have been the hottest for 500 years. Some railway tracks buckled as a result of the heat, while several road surfaces melted.

Fifteen million trees were lost as a result of the Great Storm of October 1987.

It was so cold during the winter of 1684 that the diarist John Evelyn took a coach to Lambeth across a frozen River Thames.

The Thames froze on several occasions during the 17th and 18th centuries, and to mark the occasion large markets or fairs were held on the ice. The festivities were known as the 'frost fairs'. In 1814, the year of the last of the recorded 'frost fairs', an elephant was led on to the frozen river near Blackfriars Bridge.

In December 1952, a thick smoke-laden fog – or smog – that shrouded London for four days led to the reported deaths of 4,000 people, with many dying from chronic respiratory or cardiovascular complaints.

On 14 December 1989, a tornado swept through the village of Long Stratton in Norfolk leaving a trail of devastation and a million pounds' worth of damage. Chimneys and roof tiles were ripped off buildings, car windows were smashed and a caravan was tipped on its side. Only one person was injured, though.

A rainbow lasting over three hours was reported in Wales in 1979.

The legend of St Swithun has its origins in Winchester. According to the legend, the saint's remains were moved against his dying wishes from their final resting place in the grounds of Winchester Cathedral to the inner sanctum, whereupon it started to rain for forty days as a sign of his displeasure. Now, if it rains on the saint's day, 15 July, it is said to herald another 39 days of rain.

In November 1988, strong winds in London's well-known Jewish suburb of Golders Green, blew off the last letter of the film being advertised on the front of the Cannon Ionic cinema. The title read 'Who Framed Roger Rabbi'.

GREAT BRITONS
PAST AND PRESENT

Winston Churchill's family motto was 'Fiel Pero Desdichado', meaning 'Faithful But Unfortunate'.

According to his mother, Professor Stephen Hawking was often near the bottom of the class at junior school and was late learning to read.

In 2006, fundraiser Lloyd Scott completed the London Marathon in one of the slowest times ever. Dressed as St George in armour weighing 100lb and trailing a 200lb dragon, it took him eight days and 13 minutes to cross the finishing line. In 2009, Major Phil Packer, who was told by medics he would never walk again having lost the use of both legs following a rocket attack in Iraq in 2008, astounded doctors by completing the London Marathon. He walked the 26.2 mile-course in 13 days, just one month after he first started using crutches.

The early years of Sir Isaac Newton's life did not show him to be an intellect of any great note. He was bottom of his grammar school in Grantham, and only managed to redeem this status by winning a fight in the playground.

Philip Neame is the only holder of a Victoria Cross to win an Olympic gold medal. He earned his medal at Neuve Chapelle in France in December 1914 when, in the face of heavy fire, he engaged German enemies in a single-handed bombing attack, stopping their advance for three-quarters of an hour. Ten years later he picked up the gold at the Paris Olympics as a member of the four-man team in the Running Deer (single shot) competition, where a moving target simulated the animal.

When Sir Richard Branson left school, his headmaster told him, 'I predict you will either go to prison or become a millionaire.'

Charles Darwin had a stammer.

Long before he came up with his theories on evolution, Darwin had tried to follow his father's footsteps into medicine. However, his time at Edinburgh University Medical School ended abruptly when he realised he couldn't stand the sight of blood and body parts.

Darwin was nicknamed 'Gas' at school because of his love of chemistry.

Sir Francis Drake took three years to circumnavigate the globe.

Although Julie Andrews played the original Eliza Dolittle in the Broadway musical *My Fair Lady*, Audrey Hepburn was chosen to play the part in the 1964 film. The studio executives did not want Andrews because she didn't have any film experience and thought Hepburn would be the better choice. However, while the film *My Fair Lady* took home several Oscars in 1964, it failed to win the Best Actress category. That award went to Julie Andrews for her performance in *Mary Poppins*.

When diarist Samuel Pepys was twenty-two, he survived a long and dangerous operation to have a kidney stone – said to be the size of a tennis ball – removed. He was so impressed with the stone that he carried it in his pocket everywhere, showing it to all friends and acquaintances. He also held annual dinners to show his appreciation at surviving, during which guests would drink and eat themselves into a stupor.

Contrary to popular belief, Lord Nelson, Britain's greatest naval hero, did not wear an eye-patch to hide his blind right eye, and Nelson's Column in London does not show him wearing one.

The very first Victoria Cross was awarded to Lt Charles Lucas for his phenomenally brave action in the Baltic in June 1854. During the bombardment of his ship, the HMS *Hecla*, Lucas picked up a live shell that had landed on board and hurled it overboard before it could explode, preventing any of his shipmates from coming to harm.

English philosopher Francis Bacon died in 1626 of pneumonia. He caught a chill while stuffing a chicken with snow to see if the cold would preserve it.

The first George Cross was awarded to Thomas Alderson for his action while working as an air raid warden in the Blitz in September 1940. The George Cross is the highest medal for bravery with the enemy not present.

Andrew Lloyd Webber and Tim Rice originally sold the rights to *Joseph and the Amazing Technicolor Dreamcoat* to music publisher Novello for just 100 guineas. The show went on to be performed in almost 20,000 schools or local theatres, attracting an audience of over 9 million people.

Charlie Chaplin was just nine years old when he first took to the stage as part of The Eight Lancashire Lads, a troupe of juvenile clog dancers.

Captain James Cook, the great navigator and explorer, never actually held the rank of captain. In 1775, he was promoted from the position of commander to the higher rank of post-captain.

Captain Cook was killed by Hawaiian islanders in February 1779. They believed that the power of a man was in his bones, so after they killed him they cooked part of Cook's body to enable the bones to be easily removed.

An estimated 500 million people worldwide have watched Sir David Attenborough's groundbreaking 1979 thirteen-part series *Life on Earth*.

Donald Campbell, the car and motorboat racer who broke eight world speed records during the 1950s and 1960s, is the only person to set both land and water speed records in the same year – 1964.

All of Jane Austen's novels were published anonymously.

In 1843, while performing a magic trick for his children, the great engineer Isambard Kingdom Brunel inhaled a sovereign, which eventually jammed in his right lung. After a tracheotomy failed to reach it, and unable to breathe without difficulty, Brunel sketched out a contraption to dislodge the coin. It worked.

Proms founder Sir Henry Wood was the first conductor to admit women into a major British orchestra. He was also the first person to encourage the orchestra to stand and share the applause at the end of a performance.

Mount Everest is named after the Welshman and surveyor Sir George Everest from Gwernvale, Breconshire.

Phyllis Pearsall, creator of the first *A to Z Map of London*, worked eighteen-hour days and walked 3,000 miles (4,828 km) to map the 23,000 streets of the capital in 1935. She had just one colleague, draughtsman James Duncan. Without any decent maps as a guide, she got all her information on foot.

When Tim Berners-Lee was developing what became the Internet, he first called it Enquire, because of his childhood fascination with a series of books called *Enquire Within About Everything*.

While at Oxford University, Berners-Lee and a friend were caught hacking and were banned from using the university computer.

Although now best known as founder of the scout movement, Lord Baden-Powell was also regarded as a national hero during his lifetime, after defending the town of Mafeking for seven months from the besieging Boer troops, the first real British triumph in the Boer War.

The first Brit to win a Nobel Prize was Sir Ronald Ross, who picked up the award for Physiology or Medicine in 1902 for his work on malaria.

Amy Johnson, the first woman to fly solo to Australia, was taught to fly by film star and comedian Will Hay – who was one of the first people in Britain to own a private pilot's licence.

When Johnson set off from Croydon Aerodrome on her epic journey on 5 May 1930, there was not much interest in her attempt, with only her father and a few others to see her off. By the time she had reached her first stop in Karachi she had achieved international fame.

In 2007, David Beckham insured himself for $250 million. The policy covers him for injury on the field, serious illness and disfigurement.

When, as a child, Shirley Bassey was asked to sing, she would crawl under the table and cover herself with the tablecloth before beginning.

Horatio Nelson, generally regarded as the greatest officer in the history of the Royal Navy, joined up when he was just twelve years old.

After being killed during the celebrated Battle of Trafalgar, Nelson was put into a large barrel of brandy to preserve his body during the voyage back to England. When the ship arrived back home, Lord Nelson was removed from the barrel and the crew celebrated his achievements by drinking the remaining brandy.

Queen Victoria survived seven assassination attempts.

In 1964, Dorothy Crowfoot Hodgkin became the first British woman to win a Nobel Prize – for Chemistry, for work on vitamin B-12. On reporting her award, the *Daily Mail* ran with the headline 'Oxford Housewife wins Nobel'.

Super-nurse Florence Nightingale always travelled with her pet owl in her pocket.

After returning from the Crimea War, Nightingale spent much of the remaining fifty-three years of her life in bed, suffering from a 'nervous illness'.

Former MP Tony Benn took his seat in the Commons when he was just 25.

British-born film director Alfred Hitchcock didn't have a belly button. It was sewn away following some surgery.

As a child, Hitchcock was once sent by his father to the local police station with a note asking the officer to lock him away for ten minutes as punishment for behaving badly.

While the Clifton Suspension Bridge was being built, the only way to cross it was in a basket. Designer and chief engineer Isambard Kingdom Brunel was the first to make the crossing.

In 1999, Brit Brian Jones completed the first non-stop circumnavigation by balloon, after the *Breitling Orbiter 3* completed its round-the-world trip in 15 days, 10 hours and 24 minutes.

John Napier, the brilliant 17th-century mathematician who invented logarithms and introduced the decimal point, regarded mathematics only as a hobby to be fitted in between his theological works.

Gustav Holst didn't include Pluto in his 1918 *Planets Suite*. It was not discovered until 1930.

Sir Winston Churchill was advised to join the British Army at an early age by his father, because he was not considered intelligent enough to go to university.

Sir Francis Drake and Sir Francis Chichester were both knighted, with the same sword and both by a Queen Elizabeth, for sailing around the world (Drake in 1580 and Chichester in 1967).

Sir Francis Chichester became the first person to sail single-handedly around the world, nine years after he had been diagnosed with terminal lung cancer.

Explorer Sir Ranulph Fiennes failed an audition to become James Bond, after Sean Connery. He was in the last six and had a meeting with producer Cubby Broccoli, but Broccoli said that his hands were too big and he had a face like a farmer.

Sherlock Holmes never said, 'Elementary, my dear Watson.'

THE GREAT BRITISH IN SICKNESS AND IN HEALTH

In London in the middle of the 18th century, almost 75% of children died before they reached their fifth birthday.

It was once believed that to cure a person of a fever, you should place them on a sandy shore when the tide was coming in. The waves would carry away the disease.

The British Medical Acupuncture Society is an anagram of 'Ouch, my sciatic hip. But needle art cures it.'

A 1951 army medical report confirmed that Marmite was an effective treatment for scrotal dermatitis.

A study of 10,000 civil servants by the University of Warwick revealed that those who had five hours' sleep a night or less faced a 1.7-fold increased risk in mortality from all causes, and twice the increased risk of death from a cardiovascular problem in particular, when compared with those who had seven hours' sleep a night.

Sparklers cause more injuries than any other firework.

One in four people in Britain dies from cancer.

In Tudor times, those suffering from rheumatism were encouraged to wear the skin of a donkey.

Heroin was not criminalised until January 1956. Until that time, it was a popular medicine often prescribed by family doctors.

Victorians believed smoking cleared the lungs – and struck off Dr Thomas Allinson, who founded the bakery of the same name, for describing nicotine as a 'foul poison' and advocating healthy eating.

During the Middle Ages leeches, used for medicinal bloodletting, would be found by special leech collectors who would wade into marshes and let the bloodsuckers cling to their legs.

Long before there were chemical-based remedies, athlete's foot was cured by placing thinly sliced garlic between the affected toes.

In 2003, 2,500,000,000 Paracetamol tablets were sold over the counter in the UK.

The first family planning clinic was opened by women's rights campaigner Marie Stopes in Holloway in north London in 1921.

Seven million Brits suffer from a serious skin complaint.

In the early part of the 20th century, operations to remove tonsils were very popular, often being done by GPs over the kitchen table on a Saturday morning for a nominal fee and considered a panacea for throat infections. However, the practice became less common in the early 1950s because it was noted that those who had undergone the operation were at increased risk of contracting polio.

During the Crimean War, the British army lost ten times more troops to dysentery than to battle wounds.

For many centuries it was believed that scrofula – tuberculosis of the lymph nodes in the neck – could be cured by the touch of the King of England. During his twenty-five-year reign, King Charles II is said to have touched more than 92,000 people with the disease.

Tuberculosis was responsible for approximately 20% of all deaths in England and Wales during the 17th and 18th centuries.

According to the British Snoring and Sleep Apnoea Association, 41.5% of the UK adult population snore, with 58% of snorers being between fifty and fifty-nine years of age, and men outnumbering women snorers three to one.

During World War I there were almost half a million hospital admissions for venereal disease among British troops.

In 2008, a West Yorkshire dentist was struck off the register after being found guilty of using his surgery sink as a urinal. He was also found guilty of using dental instruments to clean his ears and fingernails.

British obstetrician James Blundell performed the first successful human-to-human blood transfusion in 1818. Using the patient's husband as the donor, he took blood from his arm and, using a syringe, transfused it to the woman. Between 1825 and 1830, Blundell carried out a further ten transfusions, half of which were successful. The reason for the poor success rate of early transfusions was that the compatibility of blood was not then understood. The problem was not solved until 1900, when blood groups were finally discovered.

The world's first voluntary blood donor service began in 1921 when Percy Oliver and three other British Red Cross members became the first volunteers to give blood to patients in King's College Hospital, London. Having realised that many patients had neither friends nor relations willing to donate blood, he formed the London Blood Transfusion Service and built up a donor panel from his home.

Blood pressure complaints are the most common reason for going to the doctor in the UK.

The hardest thing in your body is the enamel on your teeth.

A total of 85% of people believe they look after their teeth well, but only 66% of people clean their teeth twice a day and nearly one-third of UK adults have twelve or more fillings.

A scientific study found that women suffering from depression may wear too much perfume because the illness damages their sense of smell.

When philosopher Jeremy Bentham died in 1832 he requested in his will that his body should be preserved and stored in a wooden cabinet. He called this his 'Auto-Icon' and was originally kept by his disciple, Dr Southwood Smith. University College, London, acquired his body in 1850 and have kept it on public display ever since. The Auto-Icon has a wax head while the real head is in a mummified-state locked away in the university. After his death, and at his request, students of the university dissected Bentham's body for medical research, and Dr Southwood Smith reassembled the philosopher's skeleton and put him in a sitting position on his favourite chair.

Most adults suffer between two and three colds each year, while children can have between four and eight.

The common cold causes more days off work or school than any other ailment.

December is the most common month for catching a cold.

More people die abruptly of a heart attack on Christmas Day than on any other day of the year.

When Sir Walter Raleigh brought potatoes and tobacco back to Britain from the New World, he received a mixed reaction. Many people believed the potatoes were a health hazard that could cause consumption and flatulence among many other ills. Tobacco was not thought to have any adverse risks, though.

In Britain, trousers cause twice as many accidents as chainsaws.

The Black Death killed around one-third of the British population between 1348 and 1350, causing many churches to run out of consecrated land for graves.

The Black Death got its name from the black blotches that appeared on the victim's skin before dying.

By 1949 it is estimated that 81% of men and 39% of women in the UK were smokers.

In 1901, the average life expectancy in the United Kingdom was forty-seven years.

If we put together all the time we spend blinking, we would 'see' blackness for 1.2 years.

It was once believed that if you stuck an elder twig in your ear and wore it day and night, you would be cured of deafness.

During the 18th century, hospitals were so rife with infections that they were often seen as a 'gateways to death'. Such were the poor chances of getting out alive, patients would have to pay a deposit on being admitted, to cover burial costs.

Records kept during World War II detailing the health of conscripted men revealed there were nine cases of men with three testicles.

The world's first test-tube or IVF baby was Louise Joy Brown, who was born in Oldham General Hospital on 25 July 1978. In May 1999, Louise's sister Natalie was the first test-tube baby to have a child of her own. Daughter Casey also made medical history and ended fears that girls born through IVF treatment would not be able to have healthy children.

More than 30,000 women a year in Britain now undergo IVF and 11,000 babies are born annually as a result.

In all, 80% of women wash their hands after going to the toilet, compared with just 55% of men.

Over 60,000 accidents involving training shoes happen every year, with another 60,000 accidents caused by slippers.

The latest UK figures also reveal that 532 accidents involved false teeth.

Vasectomies take fifteen to thirty minutes to complete.

On average, it takes eleven years of development and £500 million for each new medicine that reaches the patient.

During the Middle Ages, those suffering with tooth problems were advised by doctors to pray to St Apollonia – the patron saint of toothache.

The most common reason for going into hospital when you are not ill is childbirth.

In the UK in 2007, 2,500 people died in traffic accidents while 3,000 died from hypothermia and cold-related problems, mostly in their own homes.

Sir James Young Simpson was the first surgeon to use chloroform as a general anaesthetic, and was keen for women to use it during childbirth. There was great opposition from some sectors of the Church, however, who believed that women should not have any pain relief during labour and birth because the Bible stated, 'In sorrow shalt thou being forth children.' It was not until Queen Victoria used chloroform during the birth of her eighth child, Prince Leopold, in 1853, that its use became generally accepted.

Prescription charges were first introduced in 1952 – just four years after the NHS was set up – in order to prevent the 'frivolous use' of the health service.

Over a lifetime, the average person will breathe in around 40 lb (18 kg) of dust.

According to the Royal Society for the Prevention of Accidents, each year 1,000 people go to hospital after accidents involving Christmas trees, while a further 1,000 are hurt by trimmings or in the process of putting up decorations, with 350 injured by Christmas lights.

Every year, around 10 million prescriptions for sleeping tablets are written in Britain.

Infant mortality rates in Britain in 1900 were actually higher than in 1800.

A 2009 study by *Which? Magazine* found that 8% of people have tried to fix their own dental problems. Procedures they have tried include using household glue to stick down a filling or crown, popping an ulcer with a pin, trying to extract a tooth by using a piece of string tied to a door handle and trying to mend or alter dentures.

GREAT BRITAIN

 'Blighty', the affectionate slang term for Britain, comes from the Hindu word 'bilayati', meaning foreign, and it was used during Britain's rule of India to refer to things from the homeland. It became a popular term in World War I when a 'blighty wound' was one that was serious enough for a soldier to be sent back to Britain to recuperate.

 Rutland is the only county that doesn't have a McDonald's.

 Rutland Water is the largest artificial lake in Europe.

 It is forbidden to walk on Hadrian's Wall.

 Westward Ho! is the only place in Britain that ends with an exclamation mark.

 After London, Liverpool was the most bombed British city during World War II, with almost 1,970 tons (2,000 tonnes) of high explosives dropped in the local area.

The longest pier in Britain is Southend-on-Sea Pier in Essex, which is an amazing 2,158 m (7,080 ft) long.

The longest pub name in Britain is The Old Thirteenth Cheshire Astley Volunteer Rifleman Corps Inn, which is found in Stalybridge, Manchester. Stalybridge is also home to the shortest pub name in Britain – Q.

On April Fool's Day in 1959, the residents of Wellingborough woke to find a trail of white footprints painted along the main street of their town. At the end of the trail were the words, 'I must fly.'

Scotland got its name from the 'Scoti' or 'Scotti', a Gaelic-speaking group who came over from Ireland in around AD 500 and settled in Argyll.

There are no motorways in East Sussex.

The White Tower, the oldest and most conspicuous part of the Tower of London, got its name during the 13th century, when Henry III had it whitewashed.

Britain's largest rock salt mine in Winsford, Cheshire, covers an area of 15 square kilometres (5.8 square miles) underground, which could accommodate 700 football pitches. It has 225 km (140 miles) of tunnels and is 200 m (656 ft) deep – more than the height of Blackpool Tower.

The Crown Jewels are rumoured to have been hidden in Winsford rock salt mine during World War II, because of its constant cool temperature and cleanliness.

The library at Worcester Cathedral contains a piece of human skin, which was taken from a Viking invader and nailed to the cathedral door as a warning to other potential attackers.

Hull has no cathedral, but does have Britain's largest parish church – Holy Trinity.

The Thames contains more than eighty islands and eyots – which are small islands created by an accumulation of silt.

There are over 900 stone circles or circle sites throughout the British Isles.

Natives of Leeds are known as Loiners.

The Ridgeway in Berkshire is said to be the oldest road in the world. It has been used for 20,000 years – even before Britain separated from mainland Europe.

Birmingham's Central Library is Europe's largest public library and lends 8 million books each year.

The English city with the fewest number of letters in its name is Ely.

The Old Bell in Malmesbury is reputed to be the oldest purpose-built hotel in Britain, having welcomed guests since it first opened in 1220.

The British Library in London was founded in 1753 and holds 29 million books.

The Royal Liver Building in Liverpool was Britain's first multi-storey building with a reinforced concrete structure.

Crystal Palace, the area of south London between Dulwich, Croydon and Brixton, was named after the iron-and-glass building, designed by Joseph Paxton, that housed the Great Exhibition of 1851 and which was moved there from Hyde Park in 1854. The phrase 'Crystal Palace' was originally coined by *Punch* magazine to describe the Great Exhibition. The building was destroyed by fire on 30 November 1936.

The most popular map sold by Ordnance Survey is the Explorer map of White Peak in the Peak District.

The statue of Eros in Piccadilly Circus, London, is aligned so that his arrow points towards Wimborne St Giles, Dorset, country seat of the Seventh Earl of Shaftesbury, whose philanthropy helped raise public awareness of the plight of the poor in 19th-century England.

The total surface area of the United Kingdom is 94,526 square miles (244, 821 square kilometres).

Inverness, Brighton and Hove, and Wolverhampton were all given royal charters to celebrate the millennium, elevating them from town to city status. Preston, Stirling, Newport, Lisburn, and Newry joined the city ranks in 2002 in celebration of the Golden Jubilee of Queen Elizabeth II.

The selling of birdseed is no longer permitted in Trafalgar Square in London, as the pigeons are considered to be a health hazard.

Cardiff is the youngest capital city in Europe, having replaced Swansea in December 1955.

The shortest name of a bridge crossing over the River Thames is Kew.

The Harland and Wolff shipyard in Belfast has the world's biggest dry dock, measuring 556 x 93 m (1,824 x 305 ft).

Brennand Farm, north-west of Dunsop Bridge in Lancashire, is said to be the geographical middle of Great Britain. BT installed its 100,000th payphone at the site in 1992 and included a plaque to explain its significance. It reads: 'You are calling from the BT payphone that marks the centre of Great Britain.'

Oxford has more published authors per square mile than any other city in the world.

The first crematorium in Britain was founded in Woking in 1878, when a piece of land close to St John's Village was bought by Sir Henry Thompson, surgeon to Queen Victoria and founder of The Cremation Society. Among those cremated there were Thomas Hardy and Dr Barnardo.

The Millennium Stadium in Cardiff has the largest retractable roof of any sports arena in the world.

Stilton cheese has never been made in the town of Stilton, in Cambridgeshire, but was sold to travellers there as they passed between London and York.

Galloway Forest Park, in Dumfries and Galloway is the largest forest in the UK, covering 297 square miles (769 square kilometres).

Loch Lomond is the largest expanse of fresh water in Britain, measuring 27.5 square miles (71.2 square kilometres). However, at 22.6 miles (36.4 km) long, it is only the third longest loch in Scotland, with both Loch Awe and Loch Ness longer.

Olney in Buckinghamshire is home to the original annual pancake races. The tradition began in 1445, when a woman from the town heard the church bell calling people to prayer while she was making pancakes; she ran there in her apron, still clutching her frying pan. Competitors in today's races have to be local housewives and they must wear an apron and a hat or scarf.

Marble Arch in London, which was built by John Nash in 1827, originally stood in front of Buckingham Palace. It was moved in 1851 to Hyde Park because the state coach was unable to pass through the central arch. Commoners are still not supposed to walk through the central arch, as it remains reserved for the Royal Family.

Marble Arch itself contains three rooms, which were once used as a police station. During the Hyde Park Riots of 1855, police hid inside the rooms and surprised the rioters, capturing several of the ringleaders. The police station was finally closed in 1950.

Cornwall is the only English county to have its own language – Warlinnen. It is spoken by only 2,000 people.

The Lizard Point in Cornwall is the most southerly point on the British mainland and Lizard Village is the only mainland community on the British Isles lying south of the 50th Parallel.

On average, one dead body is found in the River Thames every week.

When a poster advertising the Wallace and Gromit film the *Curse of the Were-Rabbit* was put up in Portland in Dorset, the billings had to be changed to remove the word 'rabbit', because a local superstition has banned its use for more than 100 years. Instead, rabbits are referred to as 'underground mutton' or 'those furry things'.

RAF Manston in Kent was the most bombed British airfield during World War II.

A study found Newcastle upon Tyne to be the noisiest urban area in England, with many residents facing severe hearing and health problems. Traffic noise in the city was said to reach 80.4 decibels, the equivalent of a loud alarm clock constantly ringing in a person's ear. Torquay was found to be the quietest.

Nottingham has more than 400 man-made caves under its streets.

Hitchin Council in Hertfordshire was the first to issue black bags for rubbish collection, in 1960.

Liverpool has the largest collection of Grade II-listed buildings outside London. The city has 2,500 listed buildings and 250 public monuments.

In 1978, the Department of the Environment restricted public access to Stonehenge for the first time, to try and prevent erosion. At that time, more than 2,000 people an *hour* were visiting the site during the summer season.

The longest place name is that of the Welsh village Llanfairpwllgwyngyllgogerychwyrndrobwllllantysiliogogogoch. The name means 'St Mary's Church in the Hollow of the White Hazel near a Rapid Whirlpool and the Church of St Tysilio near the Red Cave'. It was originally called Llanfair Pwllgwyngyll, however the longer name was coined to ensure prominence for a temporary railway station that was about to become redundant following completion of the Britannia Bridge in 1850. It is said that a tailor from Menai Bridge was responsible for this fabrication, which is based on features in the nearby landscape.

Richmond Castle walls in North Yorkshire are the oldest castle walls in Britain, dating from 1080.

The White Cliffs of Dover are made of chalk and erode at a rate of 1 cm (0.4 in) per year.

England makes up around 84% of the total population of Britain, Wales around 5%, Scotland 8.5 %, and Northern Ireland (since 1921) less than 3%.

The town of Beverley, near Hull, is said to have derived its name from the number of beavers found in the area. It means 'beaver stream'.

Beverley was also the first place in Britain to establish a part-time municipal fire brigade, in 1726.

A total of 724 members of the *Titanic* crew lived within the Southampton area. Only 175 returned home to their friends and families.

Lowestoft in Suffolk is the most easterly town in England.

Salisbury Cathedral clock is the oldest surviving functional mechanical clock in the world, having been installed in 1386. It was rediscovered in the 1930s when it was described as a pile of junk in one of the Cathedral's roof spaces. It now resides in the main cathedral nave and is still in fully working order — although the side that rings only does the motions, as it has no bell to strike.

The towers of the Humber Bridge are 36 mm farther apart at the top than the bottom to take account of the curvature of the Earth.

The high-level walkways on Tower Bridge in London, which were designed so that the public could still cross the bridge when it was raised, were closed down in 1910 due to lack of use. Most people preferred to wait at the bottom and watch the bascules rise up.

One of the narrowest streets in the world is said to be in Port Isaac, Cornwall. Known as 'Squeeze-Belly Alley' is only 18 inches (46 cm) wide.

The remains of Britain's oldest house are believed to be near the village of Howick in Northumberland and are said to be 10,000 years old.

The River Swale is reputed to be the fastest-flowing river in Britain.

The building known as 'The Gherkin' at 30 St Mary Axe, which opened in 2004, was London's first eco-friendly skyscraper. Its shape allows maximum natural light and ventilation inside so it uses only half the amount of energy normally used by an office block.

Carnforth Station in Lancashire would never have become part of cinema history, by providing the backdrop for *Brief Encounter*, if it had not been for World War II. When filming took place in 1945, the threat of air raids still hung over London; the filming would be at night, with a huge lighting rig, which would not be possible in capital, prompting the film crew to move far north. The director, David Lean, chose Carnforth as the slopes up to the platforms were much easier for the actors to run up and down than stairs.

Fordwich in Kent is England's smallest town, with a population of 300.

If a person from Huddersfield spoke of a 'mullock' they would mean a mess or a muddle, while if they said you were 'dollypawed' they would mean you were left-handed.

There are more than 13,000 existing towns and cities in Great Britain that can claim to have been mentioned in the Domesday Book.

The Nutshell in Bury St Edmonds, Suffolk, is said to be the smallest pub in Britain, measuring just 5 m by 2 m (16 ft 5 in by 6 ft 6 in).

The Buckinghamshire town of High Wycombe holds a unique ceremony each year, when the new mayor of the borough begins a term of office. The incoming mayor is weighed on a huge set of 19th-century scales in full view of the public and the weight is recorded. The outgoing mayor is re-weighed, to see whether or not they have gained any weight at the expense of the town's taxpayers during their term in office.

The Isle of Ely is not an island, but is in the fen district of Cambridgeshire.

Poole in Dorset is the second largest natural harbour in the world, after Sydney.

Buried beneath Cleopatra's Needle, which was erected on the Embankment in London in 1878, are a set of coins, the morning newspaper of the day, a razor, a box of pins, four bibles in different languages, a railway guide and twelve photos of the best-looking Englishwomen of the day.

In Hull, where the telephone system used to be under the control of the city council rather than the Post Office, phone boxes were painted cream and didn't have a crown.

Wales has a population of 3 million and a sheep population of 5 million.

Although many people believe that all land to the north of Hadrian's Wall is part of Scotland, 90% of the English county of Northumberland lies on the north side of the wall.

The border between England and Scotland is 108 miles (174 km) long.

North Yorkshire is the largest county in England, measuring 8,320 square kilometres (3,212 square miles).

At high tide, the Isle of Wight is Britain's smallest county. However, at low tide the Midland county of Rutland takes the title.

The world's first railway bridge, known as the Causey Arch, was built near Tanfield in County Durham in 1727.

Cardiff was once the busiest port in the world.

York Minster has its own police force – one of only two cathedrals in the world to do so.

The islands of Orkney and the Shetlands were once part of Norway and only became part of Scotland in 1469 when Christian I, who was at that time King of Norway, pledged them against the payment of his daughter's dowry when she married King James III of Scotland. King Christian failed to pay up the agreed sum – and the islands were formally annexed to Scotland on 20 February 1472.

In 1967, Stamford in Lincolnshire became the first place in Britain to be designated a conservation area.

The island of St Kilda in Scotland does not have any rats on it.

Marie Tussaud toured Great Britain for thirty-three years before opening her waxwork museum in London in 1835. She had only come to Britain because her marriage had ended, and then found she could not return to France as the result of the Franco-English war.

The White Cliffs of Dover run for roughly 10 miles (16 km) along the south coast of England.

The smallest city in the UK is in St David's on the Pembrokeshire coast. It has a population of just 2,000.

The Peak District was designated England's first-ever national park in 1951.

If you look on a map you will find New York in Lincolnshire, Moscow in East Ayrshire, Greenland in Sheffield, Holywood in Dumfries and Galloway and Canada in Hampshire.

Scotland's most southerly point, the Mull of Galloway, is farther south than Hartlepool.

In 1539, The Game Place House in Great Yarmouth became the first building in Britain to be used as a public theatre.

The Bristol Channel has the second highest tidal range in the world, only exceeded by the Bay of Fundy in Canada.

Holme Fen in Cambridgeshire is the lowest point in Britain, at around 2.5 m (8 ft 2 in) below sea level.

The Lake District is the most visited national park in Britain, with 100 million visitors every year.

Craigievar Castle, near Alford, Aberdeenshire, was the inspiration behind Walt Disney's fairy-tale castles.

Newtown is the most common place name in Britain.

A 2008 survey by CAMRA found the most common pub name in Great Britain was The Red Lion, followed by The Crown and The Royal Oak. Completing the top ten were The Swan, The White Hart, The Railway, The Plough, The White Horse, The Bell and the New Inn.

The ten most popular house names in Britain are The Cottage, Rose Cottage, The Bungalow, The Coach House, The Barn, The Lodge, Ivy Cottage, Sunnyside, Orchard House and Woodlands.

In terms of population, the five largest cities in the UK are London, Birmingham, Leeds, Glasgow and Sheffield.

A survey in 2002 by the Ordnance Survey found Lindley Hall Farm, near Fenny Drayton in Leicestershire, to be the centre of England. Historically, Meriden in the West Midlands has claimed this title.

The last use of the stocks for punishment was in Rugby in 1865.

There are twice as many births in Milton Keynes as there are deaths.

The narrowest house in Britain can be found at 50 Stuart Street, Millport, on the island of Great Cumbrae in North Ayrshire. The house front is just 119 cm (47 in) wide.

The fountain at Whitley Court in Worcestershire is the largest in Europe.

The Crecy Window in Gloucester Cathedral is the largest-stained glass window in Britain.

The wingspan of Anthony Gormley's *Angel of the North* sculpture is 54 m (177 ft), greater than that of a Boeing 757.

The Brambles sandbank, which is midway between Southampton and the Isle of Wight, appears only once a year for little more than hour. When it does, members of the Royal Southern Yacht Club at Hamble and the Island Sailing Club on the Isle of Wight race out to it for a cricket match. The game lasts as long as the bank lasts.

Trafalgar Square in the most landed-on square on a Monopoly board.

The sign on the Oxo Tower at Blackfriars in London was added to overcome advertising restrictions, which prevented advertising along the Thames.

The ten most common street names in the UK are High Street, Station Road, Main Street, Park Road, Church Road, Church Street, London Road, Victoria Road, Green Lane and Manor Road.

Bishop Rock on the Scilly Isles is home to the tallest lighthouse in the country, standing at 49 m (161 ft).

Sheffield has more trees per person than any other European city.

A survey by an estate agents found the ten biggest factors that can put someone off buying your house are: smoking, animals, stone cladding, a dirty fridge or Aga, Seventies-style Artex ceilings, an avocado bath suite, Seventies-style carpets, ugly garden features or gnomes, modern fireplaces and chintzy decor.

Beaconsfield in Buckinghamshire has the highest annual household income of anywhere outside London, with an average of £75,000.

The Tan Hill Inn in the Pennine Valley, North Yorkshire, claims to be the highest pub in Britain at 536 m (1,759 ft) above sea level.

Cambridge University courses of study are known as 'tripos' after the three-legged stools used by BA candidates in the Middle Ages.

A 2008 study found that residents of the Shetland Islands were the fattest in the UK, with almost 16 per cent of the local population being classed as obese.

Residents of Foula, one of the Shetland Islands, still celebrate Christmas and New Year according to the Julian calendar. Christmas is marked on 6 January and New Year's Day is 13 January.

Ripon is Britain's oldest city, with a charter granted back in AD 886.

A university study recently found that the Amber Valley district of Derbyshire was the least cheerful place in England, while the residents of Bournemouth in Dorset, are said to be the happiest, with 82% saying they were content.

The name 'Graham' derives from the town of Grantham.

Grantham is home to the only living pub sign in the country. The Beehive Inn's beehive has been there for 200 years.

The tomb of the Unknown Warrior in Westminster Abbey is the only tombstone in the abbey upon which you are forbidden to walk.

Windsor Castle is the world's largest inhabited castle.

The River Usk in Wales has the second-highest tidal rise and fall in the world.

The town of Berwick-upon-Tweed in Northumberland changed hands between Scotland and England thirteen times from 1147 to 1482 before finally becoming part of England.

There are 116,000 pillar boxes in Britain.

The Royal Mail delivers 3 million poorly addressed items every day.

Bedfordshire is the smallest shire county.

The world's first garden city was built at Letchworth, Hertfordshire, in 1904.

Twenty-two new towns were built between the 1940s and the 1970s, intended to improve housing conditions for those living in the inner cities by creating utopian communities for people to live and work in. They were: Basildon, Bracknell, Crawley, Harlow, Hatfield, Hemel Hempstead, Stevenage, Welwyn Garden City, Corby, Cwmbran, Newton Aycliffe, Peterlee, Redditch, Runcorn, Skelmersdale, Washington, Milton Keynes, Northampton, Peterborough, Telford and Warrington.

The ruined keep at Bridgnorth Castle in Shropshire leans at an angle of 15 degrees, three times greater than the Leaning Tower of Pisa.

The longest river in the UK is the Severn.

Bethlehem is not only a town in Israel, but is also located along the banks of Afon Tywi in Carmarthenshire, Wales.

The University of York is said to have more ducks per square metre than any other British university.

The highest waterfall in the UK is the Eas a Chual Aluinn in Scotland, which has a drop of 201 m (659 ft).

GREAT BRITISH ROADS AND TRANSPORT

Between 1930 and 1934, there were no speed limits on Britain's roads. A 30 mph (48 km/h) general speed limit was introduced in 1934.

The first driving licence was introduced in 1903. Costing five shillings (25p), it was valid for a year, given to anyone who applied and didn't involve a driving test.

Driving tests were not made compulsory until 1935 and cost 7s 6d (37.5p), although they were suspended throughout the whole of World War II.

Roads take up less than 1% of the area of Britain.

In all, £50 billion worth of goods are shipped through Dover each year. It is the busiest port in the world.

During the last six months of 2008, more than 60,000 hand-held devices (mostly mobile phones) were left in the back of black cabs.

Breast implants, human skulls and bull's sperm were among the 170,000 items lost on London's transport network during 2008.

There are no roads in the City of London. Every road turns into a street upon reaching the City.

The M6 toll road in Birmingham was lined with 2.5 million pulped Mills & Boon novels when constructed in 2003. The novels were pulped at a recycling firm in south Wales and used in the preparation of the top layer of the motorway. The pulp helps hold the Tarmac and asphalt in place and also acts as a sound absorber.

Greenford Station is the only stop on the London Underground with an escalator that takes passengers *up* to the trains.

Thomas Bouch was originally given the job of designing the Forth Rail Bridge, however after his rail bridge over the River Tay collapsed on 28 December 1879, Sir John Fowler and Benjamin Baker were appointed instead.

Double-decker buses can lean farther to the side without falling over than human beings can because they have a lower centre of gravity.

In 1952, a London bus had to leap from one side of London's Tower Bridge to the other when the bridge began to rise with the bus still on it.

The Menai Straits Bridge and road (joining Wales to Anglesey), which was opened in 1826, was the first national road scheme paid for by the government from public funds.

Durham was the first city in Britain to introduce a congestion charge, which began in October 2002.

A 2009 survey found that Swansea's SA4 postcode area is the most likely place in the UK for drivers to make a claim for a crash or stolen car.

During the three-hour morning peak, London's busiest tube station is Waterloo, with 51,100 people entering. The busiest station in terms of passengers each year is Victoria, with 76 million.

More than a quarter of eighteen- to thirty-four-year-olds never have a road map in the car.

London traffic wardens issued 344 parking tickets on the first day parking meters went into operation on 19 September 1960.

You are allowed to drive a Routemaster bus with an ordinary driver's licence as long as you only carry eight passengers.

The first parking ticket was put on the Ford Poplar of Dr Thomas Creighton, who was treating a heart attack patient at the time. He was excused from paying his £2 fine.

Heathrow's air traffic control centre has four holding areas over southern England for aircraft awaiting permission to land.

The first-ever submarine was made in London by Dutchman Cornelius Drebbel, in around 1620. The craft was essentially two rowing boats, one turned upside down and sealed on top of the other with leather casing, and was propelled by twelve oars protruding through sealed ports in the casing. It is alleged that it was rowed from Westminster to Greenwich and back under water in three hours.

The first traffic cones were made by the Metropolitan Police during the mid-1950s. They were triangular blocks made out of wood. It was not until 1961 that the first rotationally moulded plastic traffic cone appeared on our roads.

The last horse-drawn bus ran in London on 25 October 1911.

In 1901, the first car to be insured by Lloyd's of London was covered by a marine policy. Cars were such a novelty, an underwriter wrote a normal marine policy for the car on the basis that it was a ship navigating on dry land.

It is believed that over 70% of all the original Land Rovers ever built are still on the road.

The concept of 'commuters' and 'commuting' first arose in 1842, when the Liverpool and Manchester Railway launched season tickets. They called them 'commutation tickets', since the money paid up front was 'commuted' into journeys. Although the term 'season tickets' remained the usual term in Britain, the term 'commutation tickets' became common in America, with the word 'commuter' being used there from the 1860s onwards. However it wasn't until the 1940s that the word was used commonly in Britain. The optimum commuting time is 16 minutes each way...

... however, an RAC study found British commuters have the longest journeys to work in Europe, with the average trip taking 45 minutes. That is almost twice as long as the commute faced by Italians and seven minutes more than the European Union average.

A 2008 university study found that 80% of people read during their commute, 28% work, 20% sleep and just 11% talk.

Due to the high volume of traffic, the average speed of a London taxi is just 9 mph (14 km/h).

The first British car to sell a million was the Morris Minor.

In 1977, twenty-five London Routemaster buses were painted silver to honour the Queen's Silver Jubilee.

In 1961, the E-Type Jaguar sold for £2,097, at the time half the cost of an Aston Martin and a third of the price of a Ferrari.

Belisha beacons were first introduced in 1934 by the then Minister for Transport, Isaac Hore-Belisha. They were part of Belisha's road traffic bill, which sought to cut the rising death toll on the roads.

Prior to the opening of the M6 toll, the average speed between junctions 4 and 11 of the M6 was just 17 mph (27 km/h).

Up until Westminster Bridge was opened in 1750, London Bridge was the London's only crossing over the Thames.

According to the Office of National Statistics, in 2006 63% of women and 81% of men in Great Britain held a full car driving licence. This compared with 29 % of women and 69% of men in the years 1975 and 1976. Men aged between forty and sixty-nine are the most likely to hold licences.

Prime Minister William Gladstone and philanthropist Dr Thomas Barnado both had their coffins carried by Tube.

A 2008 survey saw the Hanger Lane gyratory system, near Wembley in west London, named Britain's scariest junction. Second was Spaghetti Junction, in Birmingham, with Marble Arch and Elephant and Castle in London voted third and fourth, and the South Mimms A1/M25 interchange in Hertfordshire taking the fifth spot. Scotland was also featured, with the M8 junctions through central Glasgow in eighth position.

In 1992, Clive Richley was stopped by the police having been caught driving his Reliant Robin at 104 mph (167 km/h) along the M20 in Kent.

The Reliant Motor Company was founded by Tom Williams in 1935. Williams had worked at Raleigh in Nottingham and had been involved with their three-wheeler projects. Raleigh, however, stopped making three-wheelers and so Williams decided to make his own in the back garden of his Tamworth home. His first Reliant was completed and licensed on 1 January 1935.

A 2008 survey by the AA found that almost one in four people is unable to correctly identify Britain's road signs. The five least-known signs are those for: 'cycle route ahead', 'uneven road', 'hump bridge', 'steep hill downwards' and 'national speed limits apply'.

In all, 19.7 million tons (20 million tonnes) of earth and rock were excavated during the building of the M1 in the late 1950s. Five thousand road builders were brought to work on double-decker buses each day. The total cost of construction was £50 million.

Locomotive engineer and designer Sir Nigel Gresley considered Herring Gull, Wild Swan, Gannet and Seagull as names for the fastest steam locomotive in the world, before finally settling on the *Mallard*.

From mid-winter to mid-summer, the Forth Rail Bridge expands by almost a metre (3 ft 4 in).

The world's first underground railway opened in London on 9 January 1863. The Metropolitan Railway travelled from Paddington to Farringdon.

🐑 The first escalator on the underground system was installed at Earl's Court in 1911. To reassure the public of its safety, a man named 'Bumper' Harris, who had a wooden leg, was employed to ride up and down on it all day.

🐑 There are 109 journeys between London's Tube stations that are quicker to walk.

🐑 London's 'bendy' buses are capable of carrying 140 people at a time.

🐑 The road-safety device known as 'cats eyes' were invented by road contractor Percy Shaw in 1934. His first order was for just thirty-six reflecting studs, which were used for a pedestrian crossing in Baldon, Yorkshire. Shaw had been travelling in fog one night and was saved from going off the road by a cat whose eyes were reflected in his headlights.

🐑 Britain's first bus service began in 1825 and travelled between Manchester and Pendleton.

🐑 In 1827, Robert Cocking became the first person to die in a parachuting accident, when his early parachute design proved to be unsuccessful.

🐑 There are 2.1 people for every car in Britain.

🐑 In 2004, a Cumbrian pensioner was fined £100 for making a rude sign at a speed camera.

The 'Spirit of Ecstasy' badge that has appeared on the Rolls-Royce since 1911 was inspired by Eleanor Thornton, secretary and later lover of the Second Lord Montagu of Beaulieu. Montagu was so infatuated with Thornton that he asked her to model for an emblem to place on the bonnet of his Rolls-Royce. A mutual friend, Charles Sykes, who was an artist and sculptor, crafted a figure of her pressing a finger to her lips to symbolise the secret of their love.

The original and still-immaculate Rolls-Royce Silver Ghost has 500,000 miles (804,672 km) on the clock.

Speed cameras were first introduced on British roads in 1992 after trials on the M40 had shown just how often drivers broke the limit. Cameras capable of taking 400 snapshots on each roll of film had used up their quota in just forty minutes.

Swindon became the first town to abolish fixed speed cameras in 2008 when Peter Greenhalgh, the councillor for highways in Swindon, objected to central government receiving the cash from fines while Swindon Council had to pay for the upkeep of the cameras.

There are only two Tube stations that have all five vowels in their names: Mansion House and South Ealing.

The hovercraft began its life in 1955 when inventor Sir Christopher Cockerell tested out his idea for a craft by putting a cat-food tin inside a coffee tin. To test his 'hover' theory, he then blew a jet of air through the gap between the two tins to create a cushion of air, and the hovercraft was born.

The London Underground Film Office receives more than 100 requests per month from movie and television companies wanting to film on their trains and stations.

More new models of cars first take to the road in Bedfordshire than any other county, thanks to the Millbrook Proving Ground, which has 43 miles (70 km) of tracks for testing vehicles.

The first person ever killed after being hit by a car was Bridget Driscoll, who died on 17 August 1896. She was hit by a speeding car while crossing the grounds of Crystal Palace to watch a dancing display. The car was believed to be travelling at 4 mph (6 km/h).

The first driver ever killed in a car accident was Henry Lindfield, who died in 1898 after crashing his car into a tree.

The first air charter holiday took off from Croydon Airport in May 1932, flying to Basle in Switzerland with Imperial Airways.

The *QE2* is said to be the most misnamed ship in the world. She is *Queen Elizabeth 2*, not *Queen Elizabeth II*.

According to a *British Medical Journal* study, there is a significant increase in traffic-related accidents on Friday the 13th.

The world's first sat nav, The Plus Fours Routefinder, was actually invented in the 1920s. Designed to be worn on the wrist, it used paper maps wound around wooden rollers, which the driver turned en route. The tiny scrolls also showed the mileage and gave a 'stop' instruction at the journey's end. The device was intended to allow drivers to navigate around the UK, but with so few cars on the roads it never took off.

The Cadbury's Whole Nut chocolate bar is the biggest seller in the chocolate machines at Tube stations.

In 2004, a 1961 sparkly purple bumper car capable of reaching speeds of 90 mph (145 km/h) passed its MOT. Max Tate of Newcastle converted the vehicle, which still had its conduction pole on top and looked like any other fairground fun car. However, the only working, road-adapted dodgem in the world needed permission from the DVLA before Mr Tate could take to the road.

There are 9,815 route miles (15,795 route kilometres) of railway track in Great Britain's National Rail network, 8,919 miles (14,353 kilometres) of which are open to passenger trains. There are also 40,000 bridges or tunnels and 9,000 level crossings.

The Rotherhithe tunnel under the Thames in London was built with bends so that horses would not be able to see the light at the other end and bolt for the exit.

 Walter Arnold from east Peckham was the first person to be successfully prosecuted for speeding in 1896, after he was caught travelling at four times the speed limit – 8 mph (13 km/h) instead of 2 mph (3 km/h) – by a local policeman who had given chase on his bike. Arnold was fined one shilling plus costs.

 Registration plates for cars were first introduced in 1903, with the original A1 plate obtained by the Second Earl Russell for his 12-horsepower Napier. He is said to have queued all night to ensure that he received the first number plate.

 The Humber Bridge contains enough steel cable to stretch one-and-a-half times around the world.

 The Aston Martin was named after Lionel Martin, who won races on Aston Clinton hill near Aylesbury.

 The M25 is the world's longest ring road. Built between 1972 and 1986, it is 121.5 miles (195.5 km) long and cost an estimated £909 million to build.

 Buses in London now carry the highest number of passengers since 1968 and the number is growing at its fastest rate since 1946.

 A shortage of horses in the 1790s was one reason for the early interest in the potential of steam power.

Fashion victim Janette Benson paid an extra £10,000 for her new Mini – so it wouldn't clash with her favourite pink handbag. The trendy housewife stunned salesmen at her local dealership in Wilmslow in Cheshire, by saying she would buy a Mini Cooper S only if it were an exact colour match for her outfit.

A total of 3% of male drivers would consider giving up their wife or partner rather than their car.

At the Rolls-Royce factories in Crewe and London, the cars are always referred to as Royces. They are never called Rollers.

The Rolls-Royce radiator grille is made entirely by hand and eye – no measuring instruments are used.

Rolls-Royce founder Charles Rolls was the second person in Britain to get a flying license from the Royal Aero Club – and the first to be killed in an aeroplane accident.

The average Briton will spend two weeks over their lifetime waiting for traffic lights to change, five days looking for a city parking space and four months stuck in traffic jams.

Concorde was subjected to 5,000 hours of testing by the time it was certificated for passenger flight – making it the most tested aircraft in aviation history.

The iconic map of the London Underground was designed by Underground electrical draughtsman Harry Beck in 1933. Before Beck, London Tube maps had endeavoured to show the distance between stations. He scrapped all that and came up with an easy-to-read map – based on an electrical circuit – that ignored distances and exact geographic locations in favour of clarity.

In 1987, millionaire British businessman Richard Branson and Per Lindstrand became the first people to cross the Atlantic in a hot-air balloon, rather than a helium or gas filled balloon. They flew a distance of 2,900 miles (4,667 km) in a record-breaking time of 33 hours.

The longest journey without change on the London Underground can be made on the Central line between West Ruislip and Epping. It covers 34.1 miles (54.9 km).

London Underground has been known as the Tube since 1890, when the first deep-level electric railway line was opened. Its logo – the roundel, a red circle crossed by a horizontal blue bar – first appeared in 1908.

The air in the London Underground is approximately 10 degrees Celsius warmer than it is above ground.

A 19th-century travellers' handbook advised that women journeying on a train should put a pin in their mouths when the train entered a tunnel to stop a man from kissing them.

The longest railway tunnel in Great Britain is the Severn Tunnel. It is over 4.5 miles (7.2 km) long and would take you over two hours to walk.

When it opened in 1825, the Stockton and Darlington Railway became the world's first public steam railway to carry passengers as well as goods.

British aviators John Alcock and Arthur Whitten Brown were the first people to fly an aircraft non-stop across the Atlantic Ocean. They made their flight in 1919 having joined forces with the firm Vickers and entered a *Daily Mail* competition for the first direct transatlantic flight, with a prize of £10,000.

The very first white road lines in Britain were painted on the London to Folkstone Road, near Ashford, Kent in 1914.

The word 'timetable' was first used by the London and Birmingham Railway in 1838. It derived from the maritime 'tide tables'.

The first petrol filling station in England was built by the Automobile Association at Aldermaston in Berkshire in 1920.

The Jubilee line is the only one that interconnects with every other line on the London Underground network.

In 2005, an Oxfordshire lady passed her driving test after more than forty attempts, at the age of fifty. She had started taking driving lessons when she was seventeen.

London's black cab drivers must pass an exam known as 'The Knowledge' before they can sit behind the wheel. The Knowledge takes two years of study, and prospective drivers must memorise some 25,000 streets near central London, and learn the quickest way between points. They must also know the whereabouts of every hospital, theatre, hotel and train station.

The vehicle that most people associate with London taxis was the Austin FX-4, introduced in 1958. The model, with many modifications over the years, remained in production until 1997, making it one of the longest-running production vehicles in history.

The passenger compartment of a taxi is tall enough to accommodate someone wearing a top hat.

Although they first appeared in the 1950s, the wearing of seatbelts by drivers and front-seat passengers in a car was only made compulsory in 1983. In 1991, it became compulsory for adults to also belt up in the back seat.

Britain's worst rail accident happened on 22 May 1915 at Quintinshill in Scotland, when a passenger train collided with a wooden train carrying troops. Fire swept through the troop train killing 227 people, and leaving another 246 injured.

The UK's worst aviation disaster occurred on 21 December 1988, when Pan Am flight 103 was blown up by terrorists over the Scottish border town of Lockerbie. In total, 259 people aboard the flight and eleven on the ground died in the crash, which took place 38 minutes after take-off. The debris from the aircraft was scattered across 845 square miles (2,189 square km) and the impact reached 1.6 on the Richter scale.

The suburban rail service from Bedford to St Pancras London used to be affectionately known as the 'Bedpan Line'.

The world's first package tour was organised by Thomas Cook in 1841. He took a group from Leicester to Loughborough for a temperance meeting.

Railway pioneer George Stephenson told MPs that trains would never go faster than 12 mph (19 km/h). This was to allay public fears that higher speeds would cause mental disorders in passengers.

The number of cars and taxis on the roads in Britain has increased by 25% in just ten years – that's an extra 5.5 million in a decade.

Seventeen streets in the City of London were restricted to one-way traffic as early as 1617.

All the cars in Britain would have to be piled six high in order to fit on our motorway network at the same time.

Around 70% of train journeys taken in Great Britain either start or finish in London.

Parents around the UK are clocking up over 1,600 miles (25,750 km) per year acting as a free taxi service for their children.

Britain's first motorway was the M6 Preston Bypass, which opened in 1958. When it first opened, the road had just two lanes in each direction, with a hedge forming the central reservation and no hard shoulder.

Marylebone Underground Station was known as Great Central until 1917, while Monument was called Eastcheap until 1884 and Green Park was Dover Street until 1933.

The oldest part of the London Underground is found on the East London line. Sir Marc Brunel's twin tunnels under the Thames, which were originally opened for pedestrians in 1843, predate the first Underground railway line by twenty years.

Only 6 miles (9.7 km) out of the Metropolitan line's 41.5 miles (66.8 km) are actually under ground.

Savoy Street, just off the Strand in London, is the only street in the whole country where traffic has to drive on the right.

Around 43% of peak time trips into central London involve a rail journey. No other region in Great Britain uses rail as much as London and people in London use trains six times more than people in other cities.

At 225 miles (362 km), the M6 is the UK's longest motorway, extending from Catthorpe (junction 19 on the M1) to the A7 north of Carlisle.

Two-thirds of the price of fuel is tax.

The longest railway station platform in England is at Gloucester. At 602.6 m (1,977 ft), it is about six times longer than a football pitch.

The M62 is the highest motorway in the UK. It is 1,220 ft (372 m) above sea level near to the boundary between Lancashire and Yorkshire, close to the Pennine Way footbridge.

The longest section of motorway between junctions occurs on the M11. The distance between junction 8 and junction 9 is 15.2 miles (24.5 km). However, junction 9 only has northbound slip roads, and in a southbound direction there is an interrupted length of 17 miles (27 km) between junction 10 and junction 8.

Traffic lights were used before the advent of the motorcar. In 1868, railway signal engineer J.P. Knight invented the first traffic light, a lantern with red and green signals. It was installed in front of the House of Commons to control the flow of horse-drawn coaches and pedestrians. However, it exploded the following year, injuring the policeman who was operating it.

The first experimental system of automatic traffic lights in England was installed on a small island in the middle of Princes Square in Wolverhampton in November 1927. The experiment proved successful, became a permanent feature in October of the following year and the lights are still there today.

Over 92% of passenger travel in Great Britain is by road.

In 1971, London Bridge was purchased by an American and shipped to Lake Havasu City, Arizona, to be displayed as a tourist attraction.

The rule requiring drivers to keep to the left was passed in 1835.

The tradition of driving on the left is said to date back to the time when most men travelled by horse. As most people are right-handed, they felt safer riding (or walking) on the left, with their sword arm ready to take a swipe at any potential troublemaker.

Nowhere in Britain is more than 74.5 miles (119.9 km) from the sea.

The longest railway station seat in the world is at Scarborough station. It is 139 m (456 ft) long.

When Diana, Princess of Wales's coffin was driven up the M1, signs from a safety campaign near motorway service stations saying 'Tiredness can kill, take a break' were taken down to prevent anyone getting a photograph showing the hearse next to the sign.

GREAT BRITISH FAILURES

 Primary school teacher Liz Beattie caused outrage when she suggested at the 2005 Professional Association of Teachers' annual conference that the word 'fail' should be 'deleted from the educational vocabulary'. She said that instead, the phrase 'deferred success' would encourage a more supportive attitude in the classroom.

 Jimmy White is the only man to have appeared in more than one World Snooker Championship final without ever winning the title. He lost on six occasions, five in a row.

 The advert often considered to have been the least successful of all time was for Strand Cigarettes in 1960. It featured a lonely soul smoking a cigarette on the dark, wet, lonely streets of London. Many people stopped buying Strand Cigarettes because they thought only a loser would smoke them.

In 2005, Christopher Kelman from Didcot in Oxfordshire broke into a café. He was forced to call police however, when he got stuck in a window trying to escape.

Despite being second four times in a row from 1955 to 1958, followed by three third places before a bad crash ended his career, Stirling Moss never won the Formula One World Championships.

On Christmas Day 2003, the country waited for the *Beagle 2* space probe to make contact and reveal to us whether there was really life on Mars. However, Britain's first interplanetary space mission ended in failure when the probe failed to make contact. The mission cost £45 million.

A traffic warden in Manchester issued 101 parking tickets that had to be cancelled because he had failed to remember he was working on a Bank Holiday, when most parking restrictions do not apply.

In 1914, Horatio Bottomley, a Liberal MP who was also a less-than-honest businessman, had the perfect scheme for fixing a horse race. He bought all six horses running in a particular race in Belgium, then bribed the jockeys to finish in a certain order and placed massive bets on the race. However, the racecourse was a seaside track and the day of the race proved exceptionally foggy: not only could the jockeys not work out who was where, neither could the judges. Bottomley lost a fortune.

Eddie 'the Eagle' Edwards was working as a plasterer when he qualified, entirely self-funded, for the 1988 Winter Olympics ski-jumping competition. Edwards, some 20 lb (9 kg) heavier than the next heaviest competitor, finished last in both the 70 metre and 90 metre events. He only qualified because he was the sole British applicant. In 2003, the International Olympic Committee changed to rules to stop such wild-card entrants.

In 1993, there was no Grand National for the first time (other than due to wartime stoppages). After a false start the organisers were unable to call the horses back. Several of them completed the course and first over the line in the 'Grand National that wasn't' was Esha Ness, ridden by John White and trained by Jenny Pitman.

Golfer Colin Montgomerie has achieved five second places spread across three different major championships, but has never won a major title. He came closest in 2006, when he lost the US Open by just one stroke.

Liverpudlian duo Jemini became the shame of the nation in 2003 when they became the first British act to score 'nul points' at the *Eurovision Song Contest* in Turkey with their song 'Cry Baby'. The group blamed poor stage sound equipment for their off-key vocals.

During auditions for *The X Factor* in 2004, Simon Cowell made a bet with failed auditionee Paul Holt that he would pay him £50,000 if he had a number one single. Holt was quickly signed by a record label and released the track '50 Grand for Christmas' in December that year. He failed again. It charted at number 35.

Launched in 1985, the Sinclair C5 was a battery-powered one-seater tricycle that could reach a maximum speed of 15 mph (24 km/h), requiring pedal power for starting and uphill travel. It was designed to skirt the law requiring tax and insurance. For all its novelty value, the £200 C5 completely flopped, failing to make a fortune for inventor Sir Clive Sinclair. Only 12,000 were ever produced.

In 2004, a West End musical about Oscar Wilde that was written and directed by TV and radio presenter Mike Read closed after just one night following low bookings and poor reviews.

A woman who splashed a pedestrian as she drove through a puddle failed her driving test because the incident was technically classed as a crash. The examiner told Michelle Kelly she should have stopped and exchanged details with the man.

Jan Wass, a florist from Wrexham, suffered from swollen lips and puffy eyes for fifteen months before she discovered she had developed an allergy – to flowers. She was forced to close her shop.

A racing pigeon failed to find its way home and ended up taking a 5,000-mile (8,045-km) diversion on board the *QE2* luxury liner. Liberty, a three-year-old hen, set off with 3,000 other birds from Nantes, France, for what should have been a nine-hour race home to Derbyshire. But instead of flying back to the Peak District she landed on the cruise liner and took a detour to America and back.

In 2008, an attempt to break the world record for the largest gathering of Elvis Presley look-alikes failed when dozens of his fans arrived without a proper costume. Although over 170 people arrived in Cornwall to sing 'Viva Las Vegas' as part of the record bid, sixty-three were banned for not wearing proper attire.

GREAT BRITISH POLITICS AND POLITICIANS

Prime Minister William Gladstone always told his children to chew each mouthful of food 32 times (once for every tooth) before swallowing it, although he himself was once noted at Trinity College, Cambridge, chewing up to 75 times.

In his 1953 budget, Chancellor R.A. Butler announced that the sugar ration would be increased from 10 oz (283.5 g) to 12 oz (340 g) a week to help the nation make celebratory cakes for the Queen's coronation that year.

Charles Pelham Villiers holds the record for being the longest-serving MP in British history. He served as Liberal MP for Wolverhampton from 1835 to 1885, and for Wolverhampton South from 1885 to 1898 (becoming a Liberal Unionist in 1886) – a grand total of 63 years.

Gordon Brown was only 19 years old when he received a First in History from Edinburgh University.

Until 1512, the Royal Family lived where Parliament is now situated, but a fire forced them to move out. However, the site remained a royal palace, which is why it is officially known as the Palace of Westminster.

Before the twice-weekly Prime Minister's Question Time, Harold Wilson liked to prepare himself with two or three glasses of brandy.

MPs are prevented from surfing the Internet for pornographic and other inappropriate material in their Commons offices. Among the banned websites is that of the *Daily Sport*.

During World War II, Winston Churchill asked the prime minister of Australia to send him a live platypus to help raise his spirits. Unfortunately the creature died en route to Britain, so Churchill had him stuffed and kept him on his desk for the rest of the war.

The first ethnic minority MP to be elected was Mancherjee Bhowanggree for the Conservatives in Bethnal Green in London in 1895.

The Fifth Earl of Rosebery had to step down as prime minister in June 1895, after just fourteen months in the job, because he couldn't sleep. He was regularly driven around London in his carriage in an attempt to help him nod off. However, both this and morphine failed to do the trick.

John Prescott once bought Tony Blair a goldfish to cheer him up.

🐶 Until the 19th century, the reporting of parliamentary debates was unlawful. When the House of Commons finally relaxed its restrictions, the journalist William Cobbett engaged the services of a printer to publish his reports. The printer was Luke Hansard.

🐶 William Gladstone was 84 years old when he stepped down as prime minister in 1894 – four years older than Winston Churchill when he left office in 1955.

🐶 It was Harold Macmillan who replaced the traditional rectangular Cabinet Room table with a curved one, which allowed the PM to see everyone around the table without anyone having to lean forward.

🐶 Lily Maxwell was the first woman to vote in a parliamentary election. She was the proprietor of a small shop selling kitchenware and went to the polls in a Manchester by-election on 26 November 1867. As a ratepayer, which was itself unusual for a woman at this time, she had been put on the electoral register by mistake.

🐶 Although the Clock Tower at the Houses of Parliament is often referred to as Big Ben, this is actually the nickname of the bell housed within the Clock Tower.

🐶 Big Ben's official name is the Great Bell. It weighs 13.3 tons (13.5 tonnes), while the bell hammer itself weighs 441 lb (200 kg).

🐑 When former Deputy Prime Minister John Prescott was eight years old, he and some friends set fire to a field while playing with matches. To teach him a lesson, his father shopped him to the police.

🐑 Prescott failed his 11-plus examination and left school without gaining any qualifications.

🐑 One of Gordon Brown's first acts on becoming PM was to insist on the font for No 10 emails being changed from Times New Roman 12 to Arial 14.

🐑 The longest Budget speech was 4 hours 45 minutes, by Gladstone in 1853.

🐑 The first dog to ever dine at the House of Commons was a Chihuahua. It wore a diamond collar for the occasion.

🐑 Sir Winston Churchill is said to have existed on polyphasic sleep. This sleep pattern consists of six daily naps taken every four hours instead of one long sleep every night.

🐑 MPs always bow when approaching or leaving the floor of the House of Commons – not to the Speaker, but to the altar. It was once situated in St Stephens Chapel, which was on the site of what is now the Commons.

🐑 A third of all British legislation and 70% of our economic and social law originates in the European Parliament.

Only one chancellor has failed to deliver a Budget: Tory Iain Macleod, who died in 1970 shortly after his appointment as Chancellor.

There are more than 1,000 rooms and more than 2 miles (3.2 km) of corridors in the Palace of Westminster.

When Harold Wilson entered Downing Street on becoming PM in 1964, the first meal he ate there was fish fingers.

Former Chancellor Ken Clarke does not own a mobile phone.

In 1829 Arthur Wellesley, the First Duke of Wellington, became the first prime minister to fight a duel while in office. His opponent was Lord Winchilsea, who was opposed to Wellington's Catholic emancipation, which granted almost full civil rights to Catholics in the United Kingdom. The duel was fought in Battersea Park, with the two deliberately missed each other in firing.

In 2002, MPs signed a motion to bring cats into the Houses of Parliament to deal with the growing problem of mice.

Betty Boothroyd, the former Speaker of the House of Commons, was once a member of the high-kicking Tiller Girls.

Former PM Tony Blair ran away from school as a child. One housemaster called him 'the most difficult boy I have ever had to deal with'.

Tony Blair's fourth child, Leo, was the first child to be born to a serving prime minister since Francis Russell was born to Lord John Russell in 1849.

The Prime Minister is allowed to hold a general election on any day of the week, however it has become a convention to have it on a Thursday. The last time the election was not on a Thursday was Tuesday, 31 October 1931.

The last time the Government met outside the Houses of Parliament was in 1681, when it met for one week in Oxford.

Nearly £10 million was bet on the result of the 1997 general election, which saw New Labour come to power following eighteen years of Tory rule.

It was Britain's first prime minister, Robert Walpole, who left his London home, 10 Downing Street, to the nation.

The UK is a constitutional monarchy without a written constitution.

MP Tony Benn has kept a diary since he was nine years old. From 1966 he recorded it on tape, before moving on to video in 1974. All volumes are kept in nine purpose-built garages.

Alex Douglas-Home was the last member of the House of Lords to become prime minister.

Former PM Harold Wilson was a member of the Liberal Party before joining Labour.

Wilson was investigated three times by MI5 during the 1970s after a Russian defector claimed he was a Russian spy under Soviet control.

The last Jewish person to be prevented from taking his elected seat in the House of Commons was Alderman David Salomons, the MP for Greenwich, in 1851. Jews were finally allowed to become MPs in 1858.

James Callaghan is the only man to have held all of the three other Great Offices of State (Chancellor of the Exchequer, Foreign Secretary and Home Secretary) before becoming Prime Minister.

Callaghan is also believed to be the tallest prime minister in history, at 6 ft 1 inch (185.9 cm) tall.

In 1982, Bob – a Springer Spaniel – stood for Parliament representing The Monster Raving Loony Barking Mad Dog Party. He was owned by Lord David Sutch.

The most votes ever polled by Screaming Lord Sutch himself was 1,114 in the 1994 Rotherham by-election.

When William Pitt the Younger died in office in 1806, he had debts of £40,000. Parliament agreed to pay the sum on his behalf.

Harold Macmillan had a man from the Post Office round within two hours of his resigning as prime minister, to remove his taxpayer-funded phone.

In the 18th century, there were 98 days after Walpole when the UK officially had no prime minister. In the next century this figure rose to 192, but there were only thirteen such days in the 20th century and none so far since 2000.

Thirty-five ministers in Macmillan's government, including seven Cabinet ministers, were related to him by marriage.

The highest turnout for a general election since the war was 83.9% in 1950.

The first ever tie in a parliamentary by-election occurred in Cirencester, in 1892, when the Liberals and Conservatives polled the exact same number of votes. They had to call another election.

In the 2005 general election, 646 MPs were voted in by the public, although there are only 427 green leather seats in the House of Commons.

The distance between the Government and the Opposition sides of the House of Commons is two swords' length.

John Major's one and only Budget in 1990 was the first to be televised live.

Major left school without obtaining any qualifications.

Before entering politics, Margaret Thatcher worked as a food chemist at Lyons, where she was involved in developing soft ice cream.

One day in 1945, so many starlings settled on the minute hand of Big Ben that the clock slowed by five minutes.

In days gone by, members of both the House of Commons and House of Lords could be sent to the Clock Tower's Prison Room for misbehaving during debates. Charles Bradlaugh MP was the last person to have a stay, when in 1880 he refused to swear the oath of allegiance to Queen Victoria.

Gordon Brown is blind in his left eye.

David Lloyd George, regarded by many as the man who won World War I, was the first and only Welshman to hold the office of Prime Minister.

The Chancellor of the Exchequer is the only MP allowed to drink booze in the House of Commons, and only during the Budget speech. Winston Churchill was a brandy man, while Hugh Dalton drank milk and rum. Selwyn Lloyd liked whisky and water, while Hugh Gaitskell favoured an orange juice with a dash of rum.

Spencer Perceval is the only British prime minister ever to have been assassinated. He was shot by John Bellingham in the Members' Lobby of the House of Commons on 11 May 1812.

Winston Churchill was born in a ladies loo during a dance.

The voting age was reduced from 21 to 18 in 1969.

Oliver Cromwell was hanged and decapitated two years after his death.

Prime Minister Benjamin Disraeli was the first person to use the word 'millionaire', in his 1826 novel *Vivian Grey*. So the first millionaire was actually fictional.

In 1951, the Conservative Party won the general election, despite polling less votes than the Labour Party. The reverse happened in 1974.

Sir Geoffrey Howe, Chancellor of the Exchequer from 1979 to 1983, named his dog Budget.

When Norman Lamont was Chancellor in the early 1990s, the parliamentary briefcase that was waved at photographers outside No 11 contained a bottle of whisky, while the speech itself was carried in a plastic bag by his then aide, William Hague. 'It would have been a major disaster if the bag had fallen open,' Hague said later.

Peers never wear gloves in the House of Lords when the sovereign is present.

The last monarch to reject a law that was wanted by both Houses of Parliament was Queen Anne.

Nobody has a key to 10 Downing Street. The door only opens from the inside.

The door of 10 Downing Street has always been black, except under Prime Minister Herbert Asquith between 1908 and 1916, when it was dark green.

Until the 20th century, prime ministers who lived in Downing Street used to bring their own households with them, from bedding and crockery to paintings. They would arrange their possessions in the state rooms on arrival and move them out when they left office.

The last election in the UK to be conducted with open voting records was the Oldham by-election on 4 June 1872, which had been caused by the death of Liberal MP John Platt.

William Pitt the Younger is Britain's youngest-ever prime minister. He was just twenty-four years old when he took office in 1783.

The first woman elected to parliament was Countess Constance Markievicz in 1918 for Sinn Fein. She did not take her seat. The first woman elected who did take her seat was Nancy Astor in a by-election in 1919. Astor had campaigned using the slogan 'Vote for Lady Astor and your children will weigh more.'

The Houses of Parliament were almost completely destroyed by a fire in 1834. The building we know today was not completed until 1870.

The smallest constituency is Western Isles in Scotland. The largest is the Isle of Wight.

William Gladstone spent £83,000 of his own money on rehabilitating London prostitutes.

Neville Chamberlain went to his formal appointment as PM at Buckingham Palace uncertain about whether or not the term 'kiss hands' was literal or metaphorical. It was only when the King invited him to sit down, without offering a hand, that Chamberlain worked out the answer.

When Chamberlain flew to Germany for his infamous meeting with Hitler in 1938, it was the first time he had ever been on an aeroplane.

Robert Cecil, the Third Marquess of Salisbury, was the last serving prime minister to also be a member of the House of Lords. Unlike lords today, he did not have to renounce his peerage in order to take up his seat in the Commons.

Cecil is said to have been the inspiration for the expression 'Bob's your uncle'. In 1887, he unexpectedly promoted his nephew Arthur Balfour, a man of questionable ability, to the vital front line post of Chief Secretary for Ireland. This piece of nepotism led some to say that such appointments come easily if 'Bob's your uncle'.

Balfour went on to become Prime Minister, and was the first PM to own a car.

Before the Government Hospitality Fund was set up in 1908, prime ministers employed their own servants for entertaining at Downing Street.

GREAT BRITISH ROCK AND POP TRIVIA

Bee Gee Robin Gibb has never watched *Saturday Night Fever* all the way through.

The cake on the front of The Rolling Stones' *Let it Bleed* album was baked by Delia Smith.

Scottish singer K.T. Tunstall only made her television debut on *Later...with Jools Holland* because scheduled artist Nas pulled out at the last minute. She was given just 24 hours' notice to prepare for the performance. The performance was so successful that her album, which had previously reached number 73 in the charts raced up to number 3, and she became an international star.

Former Sugababe Keisha Buchanan used to practise her singing when she was younger by recording her voice on a tape recorder, as her parents couldn't afford singing lessons.

There were only two British artists in the first UK music chart, which was published on 14 November 1951. Vera Lynn had three entries in the Top 12 with 'Forget-Me-Not', 'The Homing Waltz' and 'Auf Wiedersehen Sweetheart', while Max Bygraves was at number 11 with 'Cowpuncher's Cantata'.

'My Way' by Frank Sinatra has clocked up more weeks in the UK singles charts than any other – notching up an incredible 124 weeks since first appearing in 1969. Second is Judy Collins' version of 'Amazing Grace', which stayed for sixty-six weeks and third is 'Relax' by Frankie Goes to Hollywood, which spent fifty-nine weeks in the chart.

Girls Aloud star Nadine Coyle first found fame in 2001 when, while still at school, she entered the Irish version of the talent show *Popstars*. As one of the winners of the show, Coyle was selected to become a member of the band Six. However, when it was revealed she was only sixteen, below the stipulated minimum age of eighteen, she was disqualified from the show.

The album that has remained longest in the UK chart is *Rumours* by Fleetwood Mac, having spent 477 weeks in the chart since first entering in 1977. Meat Loaf's *Bat Out of Hell* is second with 473 weeks and third is Queen's *Greatest Hits* with 439 weeks.

Alesha Dixon only got into music after being approached on a train by a record producer, who asked her if she could sing. She had previously intended to train as a PE teacher.

Jimmy Osmond is the youngest person to have had a UK number one single, aged nine years and eight months, with 'Long Haired Lover from Liverpool' in 1972.

The Animals' 1964 single 'House Of The Rising Sun' was the first number one to have a playing time of more than four minutes.

Coldplay are named after a psychology book called *Child's Reflections, Cold Play*.

Duffy was asked to leave her school choir because her voice was 'too big' and she 'didn't fit in'.

Cliff Richard's first recording was a £10 demo disc of 'Lawdy Miss Clawdy' and 'Breathless'.

Simon Cowell turned down the chance to sign Take That because he thought Gary Barlow was too fat.

Charlotte Church's first public performance came aged just three when she sang 'Ghostbusters' at a holiday camp in Caernarfon. She had to be dragged from the stage when she refused to leave.

When the first download chart was published in 2004, the first download number one was Westlife's 'Flying without Wings'.

A total of 1.1 million copies of 'Teletubbies Say Eh-Oh' by The Teletubbies were sold in 1997.

🐶 'Unchained Melody' has been a UK number one hit for four different acts – Jimmy Young, The Righteous Brothers, Robson and Jerome and Gareth Gates.

🐶 Tommy Steele, regarded as Britain's first great rock 'n' roll idol, was also the first rock 'n' roll star to be made into a waxwork at Madame Tussauds.

🐶 Robbie Williams has won the most ever BRIT awards to date. His fifteen gongs include four with Take That. Annie Lennox has notched up the most for a female artist with seven – one for The Eurythmics – while U2 top the band list, also with seven.

🐶 Jamiroquai are the biggest BRITs losers, with fifteen nominations to date without ever actually winning one.

🐶 Britney Spears's family comes from Tottenham in north London.

🐶 The first CD to sell a million copies was Dire Straits' *Brothers in Arms*.

🐶 'Bohemian Rhapsody' by Queen is the only single to be replaced at the top of the charts by a song whose title featured a lyric from the song it supplanted: 'Mamma Mia', by Abba.

🐶 'It's Not Unusual', which topped the charts in 1965 for Tom Jones, featured a pre-Led Zeppelin Jimmy Page on guitar. The song was originally written for Sandie Shaw.

Sir Paul McCartney once hired three jets, at a cost of £28,000, to spray dry ice into the clouds above a concert at St Petersburg's Palace Square, to stop it raining while he played.

The line 'four thousand holes in Blackburn, Lancashire', which featured in the 1967 Beatles track 'A Day in the Life', came from an article read by John Lennon in the *Daily Mail* that reported 'one-twentieth of a pothole' for every Blackburn resident in the streets.

Ringo Starr is a left-handed drummer who uses a right-handed drum kit.

Take That's Gary Barlow released his first single, 'Love Is In The Air', at the age of eighteen under the stage name Kurtis Rush.

Enya was born Eithne Ní Bhraonáin.

Britain's highest-scoring Eurovision entry was the 1976 winner 'Save all Your Kisses for Me' by Brotherhood of Man, which polled 164 out of a possible 204 points.

The UK holds the record for the biggest winning margin by a Eurovision winner. Katrina and the Waves were 70 points clear of the second placed act when they took the title in 1997 with the song 'Love Shine a Light'.

The prize for the shortest performance by a Eurovision contestant also goes to the UK. In 1957, Patricia Bredin's rendition of 'All' lasted just 1 minute 52 seconds.

Girls Aloud hold the record for the shortest time between formation and reaching number one in the UK charts, with their début single 'Sound of the Underground'.

Phil Collins is only 5 ft 6 inches (167.6 cm) tall.

Elton John's 'Candle in the Wind 1997', remains the best-selling single of all time, with worldwide sales said to exceed 37 million.

Elton John's 1978 instrumental piece 'Song for Guy' was inspired by seventeen-year-old Guy Burchett, who was killed while working for John's Rocket Records as a motorcycle courier.

On 18 February 2009, Elbow received the award for Best British Group at the BRIT Awards from actor and singer David Hasselhoff. This was their first BRIT award and came nineteen years after they formed.

Helen Shapiro was the youngest female solo singer to have a number one, when 'You Don't Know' topped the chart in 1961. She was just 14 years 10 months and 13 days old, almost a year younger than Billie Piper who was aged 15 years 9 months and 20 days when 'Because We Want To' reached number one in 1998.

Twins Craig and Charlie Reid, better known as The Proclaimers, were given the nickname 'eight eyes' at junior school.

'Lola' by The Kinks was banned by the BBC when it was first released in 1970, not because of its references to a transvestite, but because the mention of 'Coca-cola' was against the corporation's policy on product placement. The ban was lifted when the song was re-recorded using the words 'cherry-cola'.

George Michael wrote the pop classic 'Careless Whisper' when he was just seventeen years old.

James Blunt wrote and recorded the song 'Goodbye My Lover' in *Star Wars* star Carrie Fisher's bathroom.

Kaiser Chiefs are named after the South African football club that former Leeds United defender Lucas Radebe played for.

In 2004, Ronan Keating entered *Guinness World Records* for being the only artist ever, in UK chart history, to have 30 consecutive Top 10 singles.

Amy Winehouse was expelled from the Sylvia Young Theatre School aged fourteen for 'not applying herself' and for piercing her nose.

The Pet Shop Boys were originally known as West End.

At the same time that Ringo Starr received an offer from Brian Epstein to join The Beatles, he was also asked to join another Liverpool group called Kingsize Taylor and The Dominoes. Ringo chose the one offering the best wage: £25 a week.

Robbie Williams has appeared more times on the UK's *Now That's What I Call Music!* series than any other artist. In the first 71 *Now!* albums he has featured 29 times, including four times with Take That.

During The Rolling Stones last world tour, lead singer Mick Jagger had an on-stage autocue to act as a prompt in case forgot any of the lyrics to band's classics songs. The screen also reminded him the name of the city in which he was performing.

The Stereophonics were originally a cover band called Tragic Love Company.

Lily Allen attended 13 schools as a child, and was expelled from several for smoking and drinking.

Downloads outsold singles in the UK for the first time in January 2005.

Mark Owen was working for Barclay's Bank when he auditioned for Take That.

GREAT BRITISH
SPORTS AND
SPORTSPEOPLE

When Kazimierz Deyna was transferred from Legia Warsaw to Manchester City in November 1978, the £120,000 transfer fee was paid for mainly in goods, including typewriters and medical equipment.

Since the Premier League was founded in 1992, only seven teams have played every season in the top flight. They are Manchester United, Chelsea, Arsenal, Aston Villa, Liverpool, Everton and Tottenham Hotspur.

Croquet was the first outdoor sport to allow both sexes to play the game on an equal footing.

Between 7 May 2003 and 24 October 2004, Arsenal Football Club went unbeaten for forty-nine games in the Premiership. They earned 121 points out of a possible 147.

Marbles were introduced into Britain by the Roman in the 1st century AD.

The first record of a game of football in Britain was written by William Fitzstephen in 1170. However, no rules were devised until 1848.

The world's first international rugby game was played in 1871 between Scotland and England. Scotland won.

Prior to 1878, football referees did not use whistles – they just waved a handkerchief, and sometimes had difficulty keeping control of the game.

Baseball was played in Surrey in 1755.

The first keep-fit class for housewives was held in Sunderland in 1929.

BBC Sports presenter Gabby Logan represented Wales in the rhythmic gymnastics team in the 1990 Commonwealth Games.

If the 1966 World Cup Final had still been level after extra time, the result would have been decided on the toss of a coin.

Former England rugby captain Lawrence Dallaglio sang in the backing choir on Tina Turner's 'We Don't Need Another Hero'.

The first-ever cricket Test triple century was achieved by Andy Sandham of England against the West Indies in 1930 in the first Test series hosted in the West Indies.

Tennis attracts the third largest amount of money in betting, after football and racing. In 2007 alone nearly half a billion pounds was staked on Wimbledon through just one betting exchange.

Despite being in England, the football team in Berwick – Berwick Rangers – plays in the Scottish League, the only English team to do so.

English-born Billy Midwinter is the only man ever to have played at Test level for both Australia and England against the other. He played eight Tests for Australia before going on to represent England in a further four during the 1870s and 1880s.

In 1929, England cricketer George Gunn was recalled at the age of fifty to tour the West Indies – seventeen years after his last Test.

During the late 1950s, Lincoln City Football Club had a centre-half named Ray Long who was over 6 ft (183 cm) tall, and a left winger called David Short, who was only 5 ft 4 inches (161.5 cm).

Glasgow Rangers have won their country's league title more often than any other club in the world, with fifty-one victories.

David Beckham was so upset at England being knocked out of the 2006 World Cup that wife Victoria bought him a belt worth over £15,000. The belt is made of titanium and white gold and adjusts automatically to fit your waist after a big meal. There are only eighty-eight such belts in existence.

Beckham will only wear each pair of his trainers once.

The Calcutta Cup, which has been competed for by the England and Scotland rugby union teams since 1879, was named after the Calcutta Football Club, which disbanded in 1877. The club's funds were withdrawn and converted into silver rupees, which were melted down to make the trophy.

Blackburn player Bob Crompton holds the record for winning most England football caps without playing at Wembley. He played forty-one times for England between 1902 and 1914; however, the stadium was not built until 1923.

Iron Maiden's Bruce Dickinson was once ranked seventh in the UK at fencing.

There were so many injuries during 2004's Women's National Festival of Rugby in Staffordshire that emergency services declared it 'a major incident'. Ten ambulances and a helicopter were needed to deal with ruptured muscles, broken bones and a dislocated hip.

When Sir David Attenborough was Controller of BBC2 during the late 1960s, he was responsible for bringing snooker to television.

Grand National fence Becher's Brook got its name from Captain Martin Becher, who rode in the very first National in 1839. His horse hit a fence, throwing Becher into the brook on the other side. For safety's sake he had to stay under the water until the rest of the field had passed overhead. He didn't compete in the race again.

Everton, Aston Villa and Fulham football clubs were created from Sunday school teams.

During her record-breaking 94-day solo round-the-world trip in 2005, Ellen MacArthur survived on only five-and-a-half hours' sleep a day, which was divided into short naps of just 36 minutes.

In 1939, just before World War II broke out, the transfer record for a football player went to Bryn Jones, who moved from Wolverhampton to Arsenal for £14,500.

If a player is sent off during the FA Cup Final, the FA can withhold his commemorative medal.

Pictures of then Deputy Prime Minister John Prescott playing croquet at his official residence, Dorneywood, in 2006, while supposedly running the country, led to a 300% surge in sales of croquet sets at Asda.

The Marquess of Queensberry Rules, on which the modern sport of boxing is based, were not devised by the Marquess in 1867, but by Welshman and boxing fan John Graham Chambers. John Sholto Douglas, the Eighth Marquess of Queensbury, was just a friend of Chambers who agreed to sponsor the regulations, which led to them being known as the Queensberry Rules.

The greatest number of finishers in a Grand National race was 23 in 1984; the fewest was two in 1928.

Squash was devised by pupils at Harrow School during the 19th century. They had the first-ever purpose-built squash courts erected during the 1860s.

After retiring from athletics, double Olympic decathlon gold medallist Daley Thompson played professional football for Mansfield Town FC.

Match of the Day's first female commentator was Jacqui Oatley, who made her début appearance on 21 April 2007.

During the football World Cup in 2006, 1.5 million flags of St George were sold.

Caps were first introduced into international football in 1886, when the English Football Association announced that all players who took the field for England in future internationals would be presented with 'a white silk cap with red rose embroidered on the front'. The rest of the world followed suit.

Cross-country running developed during the 17th century in England, when members of the aristocracy began wagering bets on the outcome of their servants racing on foot across their vast estates.

Formula One driver Jenson Button failed his driving test the first time he took it. His examiner revealed he had nipped in between two cars 'through a gap that wasn't there'.

Racing driver Stirling Moss won the British Lawnmower grand prix twice during the 1970s.

On 21 April 1997, 'Rocket' Ronnie O'Sullivan made the fastest maximum break ever recorded. It took him just 5 minutes 20 seconds to clear the table while notching up the 147.

When the urn containing cricket's famous Ashes was last taken to Australia in 2006, it was given VIP treatment with a first-class seat and security guards.

In 1964, World Cup football legend Sir Bobby Moore was treated for testicular cancer. He kept his illness a secret and went on to win that year's FA Cup with West Ham, and was also named Football Writer's Association Football Player of the Year.

Tennis star Andy Murray was a pupil at Dunblane Primary School during the Dunblane Massacre of 1996, in which Thomas Hamilton killed seventeen pupils and staff before turning one of his four guns on himself. Murray had taken cover in a classroom.

The start of the Fifth Test between England and South Africa at Kingsmead, Durban, in 1931 was delayed by 20 minutes due to the unavailability of the correct size of bails.

In 2005, snooker legend Jimmy White changed his name by deed poll to James Brown while playing at that year's Masters Snooker Final, following news that the brown ball in all major tournaments is to be backed by HP Sauce.

Wales has qualified for the football World Cup only once – in 1958.

🐾 Sheffield Wednesday only came to be formed because the Wednesday Cricket Club, who used to meet at the Adelphi pub in Sheffield, wanted to keep fit during the winter months. The called themselves 'Wednesday' because that was the day the local steel workers who formed the club took their half-day off from work to play sport.

🐾 In 2008, footballer David Pratt got his name in the record books for the wrong reasons after getting the world's fastest-ever red card. The 21-year-old striker for non-league Chippenham was sent off after only 3 seconds for a lunge at Bashley's Christopher Knowles.

🐾 The Open is the oldest of all the golfing majors, having been first held in 1860 at Prestwick Golf Club.

🐾 The last team to win Scotland's premier league title that wasn't Celtic or Rangers was Aberdeen, back in 1985.

🐾 World Cup Willie, the Union Jack-wearing British lion that was the mascot for the 1966 competition, was the first World Cup mascot and one of the first mascots to be associated with a major sporting competition.

🐾 The record number of appearances in the Grand National is eight, by Manifesto between 1895 and 1904. The horse won in 1897 and 1899, and was third in 1900, 1902 and 1903. His final appearance was at the ripe old age of sixteen, when he came eighth.

🐾 The winner of the first Grand National, held in 1839, was the five-to-one favourite Lottery, ridden by Jem Mason.

The Derby gained its name after the Twelfth Earl of Derby and Sir Charles Bunbury tossed a coin to decide after whom the Classic would be titled.

The hottest-ever Derby favourite, the 40–95 chance Surefoot, only made it into fourth position in 1890.

Footballer John Barnes was nicknamed 'Digger' during his days at Liverpool, not because of his fondness for gardening, but because his initials are JCB: John Charles Barnes.

The Stableford system of scoring golf was invented in 1931 by Dr Frank Stableford of the Wallasey & Royal Liverpool Golf Clubs, and the first competition under Stableford Rules was played on 16 May 1932 at Wallasey.

No English manager has ever won the Premier League.

Matthew Webb became the first person to swim the English Channel on 24 August 1875, when he completed the crossing in 21 hours and 45 minutes, aged twenty-seven. He died just eight years later while attempting to swim across the Niagara River below the Niagara Falls. He had been tempted by a prize of £12,000, but was swept away by the currents and drowned.

The most successful day of the year to swim the Channel is 28 August, with forty-seven people going the whole distance on that date.

Alison Streeter from Dover has successfully swum the Channel on forty-three occasions.

Norwich City Football Club's song 'On the Ball, City' is believed to be the oldest football anthem still being sung today.

The youngest person to have swum the Channel was Thomas Gregory from Eltham Swimming Club, who was just 11 years, 11 months old when he completed the swim (in 11 hours, 54 minutes) on 6 September 1988.

Sir Stanley Matthews was the first professional footballer to be knighted. His professional career lasted thirty-three years and by the time he retired in 1965, aged fifty, he had made nearly 700 League appearances for Stoke City and Blackpool and had played for England fifty-four times. He was knighted the same year.

The word 'snooker' was originally used as a slang term for new recruits at the Woolwich Military Academy.

Pretty Polly tights were named after the racehorse who won the British Fillies' Triple Crown in 1904.

In 2003, a chip-shop owner from Leeds was forced to get rid of his red forks because they reminded local fans of Manchester United. The owner of the shop near the Elland Road ground realised many customers he had were choosing to use their hands rather than the forks provided, while others were boycotting the shop completely. He changed to wooden forks.

The current marathon distance of 26 miles 385 yd was set for the 1908 London Olympics so that the course could start at Windsor Castle and end in front of the Royal Box at White City stadium.

In 2008, Harrogate Cricket Club in North Yorkshire banned its players from hitting sixes – on health and safety grounds. Players were warned that if they hit balls over the boundary without bouncing it would count only as a four.

The FA Cup's longest tie lasted for eleven hours. Alvechurch needed six games to knock out Oxford City in the fourth qualifying round in 1971, the scores being 2-2, 1-1, 1-1, 0-0, 0-0 and 1-0.

It was not until the 116th FA Cup Final match that a player was sent off. Manchester United's Kevin Moran was dismissed by referee Peter Willis for a late tackle during the match against Everton in 1985.

Rugby League came into being in 1895 following a meeting of twenty-one Yorkshire and Lancashire clubs in Huddersfield, regarding a dispute with the RFU over compensating working-class players for wages lost while playing the game. The RFU banned the payments, saying it was a breach of amateurism, so the clubs formed the Northern Rugby Football Union, which became the Rugby League.

John Surtees is the only man to ever win a World Drivers' Championship on both two and four wheels. When he was crowned World Driver's Champion at the wheel of a Ferrari in 1964, he already had seven motorcycle world championships to his name.

The first Wembley FA Cup Final had an official attendance of 126,047.

No player wears the Number 12 shirt at Portsmouth Football Club. The shirt was retired in honour of the club's fans, who are regarded as the twelfth man on the pitch.

Leicester City are the FA Cup's biggest losers, having made it to the FA Cup Final the most times without going on to win the trophy. They have reached the finals four times in the history of the FA Cup and lost on every occasion, the last time being in 1969.

Blackburn Rovers owe their name to its lowly beginnings in 1875. The team didn't have an official ground for quite some time after their formation, causing them to be dubbed the 'Rovers'.

Rowing legend Sir Steve Redgrave was the first athlete to win gold medals in five consecutive Olympics. He won his fifth gold by a margin of 0.38 seconds.

Redgrave was also a member of the 1989–90 British bobsleigh team.

The only Olympian ever to be awarded the Nobel Peace Prize was Philip Noel-Baker of Great Britain, who won the silver in the 1500 metres at Antwerp in 1920.

David Beckham once earned just £2 a night collecting empty glasses at Walthamstow dog track.

The first Littlewoods Pools coupon attracted only 35 punters.

There have been six sinkings during the annual Oxford and Cambridge University Boat Race, but the race result has only been determined by a sinking on three occasions: Cambridge twice, in 1859 and 1978, and Oxford once, in 1925. On 31 March 1912, both boats sank and the race was held again the next day. On March 24 1951, Oxford sank and the race was rescheduled for 26 March, when Cambridge won.

The heaviest oarsman ever to compete in the Boat Race was Thorsten Engelmann, the stroke man of the 2007 Cambridge Blue Boat, who weighed in at 17 st 6 lb (110.7 kg).

The closest finish in Boat Race history came in 1877, when the event was declared a dead heat. However, the smallest winning margin stands at just 1 ft (30 cm), set when Oxford pipped Cambridge in 2003.

Three-times Olympic Gold medal winner Chris Hoy was inspired to cycle after watching the film *E.T.*

The modern sport of bungee jumping was founded in 1979, not in Australia or New Zealand but from the Clifton Suspension Bridge in Bristol.

The World Marbles Championships takes place every Good Friday in the car park of The Greyhound pub in Tinsley Green, West Sussex. The village, near Crawley, is reputed to have been the scene of an epic marbles battle in Elizabethan times over the hand of a local maiden.

Grimsby Town are the only British football team never to have played in their home town. The ground Blundell Park is in neighbouring Cleethorpes.

In spring 1963, a Plymouth Argyle Football Club match was watched by an incredible 100,000 people. The team were on a mini tour of Poland and were asked to play a game as a warm-up for an international cycle race. It was their biggest-ever crowd.

Lewis Hamilton was named after the US Olympic gold medallist Carl Lewis.

Hamilton's first driving victory came at the age of six, with a radio-controlled car in a Blue Peter competition.

You are not allowed to play polo left-handed.

England's Rugby Union ground at Twickenham is nicknamed Billy William's Cabbage Patch, as it was formerly the site of a market garden, before being bought by Williams, who turned it into a rugby pitch.

🐶 Quarter-finalists at Wimbledon get free tea at the tournament for life.

🐶 The shortest person to ever compete at Wimbledon was Miss C.G. Hoahing, who was just 4 ft 9.5 inches (146 cm) tall.

🐶 Britain's Andy Green has held the Land Speed Record since 1997, when his *Thrust SSC* reached 763.03 mph (1,227.98 km/h).

🐶 Ian Botham, Dennis Compton, Geoff Hurst and Phil Neale have all played professional football and first-class cricket. Botham for Scunthorpe and Somerset, Compton for Arsenal and Middlesex, Hurst for West Ham and Essex, and Neale for Lincoln City and Worcestershire.

🐶 The England rugby team always includes a lawyer in the tour party.

🐶 When Blackburn Olympic beat the Old Etonians in the 1883 FA Cup Final, one of their supporters was overheard to say the trophy was 'nowt but a teapot'.

🐶 Women were not allowed to compete in the modern Olympics until the second games of 1900. The first woman to receive an Olympic gold medal was Charlotte Cooper, a tennis player from Middlesex, who went on to win Wimbledon five times.

🐶 Only three teams have won the FA Cup without conceding a single goal during the entire competition: The Wanderers, who won in 1873, Preston North End in 1889 and Bury in 1903.

Swindon Town are the only League football club whose name shares no letters with the word 'mackerel'.

The names of football clubs Aston Villa, Liverpool, Northampton Town, Charlton Athletic and York City all start and end with the same letter.

The last team to win the FA Cup with an all-English team were West Ham in 1975.

Cardiff City are the only non-English club to win the FA Cup, beating Arsenal 1-0 in the 1927 final at Wembley. In fact, the trophy was generally known as the English Cup until the Welsh team's victory.

While leading the 1934 US Open, Scottish golfer Bobby Cruickshank knocked himself out when he threw his club into the air in celebration of a good shot. He finished joint third.

The new Wembley Stadium pitch is 4 m (13 ft 1 in) lower than the previous pitch. Also, there are 107 steps in the trophy presentation route, while the old stadium had just thirty-nine steps.

The Test match between England and South Africa at Durban in 1939 was abandoned as a draw on the tenth day because the England players had to catch their boat home.

Allen R. Astles, representing the University of Wales, potted 10,000 tiddlywinks in 3 hours, 51 minutes, 46 seconds in Aberystwyth, Dyfed, in February 1966.

The fastest time in which one tiddlywink has been squidged over a 1-mile (1.6-km) course is 52 minutes, 10 seconds by the pairing of James Cullingham and Ed Wynn, in Stradbroke, Suffolk, on 31 August 2002.

Liverpool Football Club don't have a mascot.

W.G. Grace was just nine years old when he played his first competitive cricket match for West Gloucestershire.

Golf was outlawed in Scotland in 1457 by James II, who was preparing to invade England and wanted his people to concentrate on useful hobbies like archery. The ban was eventually lifted in 1502.

Royal Ascot dates from 1711, when Queen Anne drove from nearby Windsor with her entourage for a day's sport organised at her command.

A ban on divorcees entering the Royal Enclosure at Ascot was lifted in 1955; however, undischarged bankrupts are still unwelcome and admission of ex-prisoners is at the discretion of officials.

Crystal Palace is the only one of the English league clubs whose name begins with five consonants.

The first recorded instance of a game of conkers being played in Britain was in 1848.

J.W.H.T. Douglas was the only England cricket captain ever to have four initials.

Sherlock Holmes creator Arthur Conan Doyle popularised skiing in Switzerland.

Conan Doyle was also a founder and the first goalkeeper of Portsmouth United Football Club.

Hull City is the only football club in the top four football leagues whose name contains no letters you can colour in.

In the 1908 Olympics, the gold medal in the Tug of War event went to the City of London Police, with Liverpool Police taking the silver and the K Division Metropolitan Police taking the bronze.

GREAT BRITISH WORDS AND PHRASES

The dot over the letter 'i' is called a tittle.

The Oxford English Dictionary lists about 615,000 words. Of those, it's estimated that about 200,000 words are in common use, which is twice the number of those used by the French.

The most-used letter in the English language is the letter 'E'; the least used is the letter 'Q'.

The phrase 'white van man' was first coined in 1997 by BBC Radio 2 presenter Sarah Kennedy.

When a Leicestershire man asks for a 'croggy', he wants a lift on your bike.

The word 'latchstring' contains more consonants in a row than any other English word.

During the 17th century, the toilet was often politely referred to as the 'necessary house'.

The word 'testimony' has its origins in the word 'testicles' and dates from Roman times, when only men could give evidence in court.

'Acre' comes from the old English word 'aecer', which means 'ploughed field'. It was defined as the area a group of oxen could plough in one day.

According to *The Oxford English Dictionary*, the phrase 'cool Britannia', which is used to describe the contemporary culture of the United Kingdom during the 1990s, was actually first coined by 1960s group the Bonzo Dog Doo-Dah Band. It was the title of the opening track on their 1967 album *Gorilla*.

Meanwhile, the phrase 'girl power', so often associated with The Spice Girls, also has earlier roots, having first been used by the novelist Malcolm Lowry in his 1952 book *Under the Volcano*.

'Typewriter' is the longest word that can be made using the letters on only one row of the keyboard.

There are more than 140 euphemisms for being drunk in the English language.

'Stewardesses' is the longest English word that is typed with only the left hand.

'Jitty', 'jennel', 'ginnel', 'twitchel', 'twitten', 'bacskie', 'wynd', 'close', 'entry' and 'eight-foot' are all words that are used to describe the walkway between houses.

'Lollipop' is the longest word typed with the right hand.

'Humpty Dumpty' was a colloquial term used in 15th-century England describing someone who was obese.

'Pneumonoultramicroscopicsilicovolcanoconiosis', meaning a lung disease caused by inhaling fine silica dust, is the longest word in the English dictionary. It contains forty-five letters.

At thirty-four letters, 'Supercalifragilisticexpialidocious', meaning 'wonderful' and coming from the song of the same name that appeared in the 1964 film *Mary Poppins*, is the longest non-medical term.

The 'Alice band' got its name from the girls' headband worn by the title character in Lewis Carroll's books. It was the illustrator John Tenniel who was responsible for creating her look, which included the hair accessory.

The sentence 'The quick brown fox jumps over the lazy dog' contains every letter of the alphabet.

The word 'no-mark' was first recorded in the Channel 4 soap *Brookside*.

'Dreamt' is the only English word that ends in the letters 'mt'.

When the compact edition of *The Oxford English Dictionary* was introduced, it was sold in a case that also included a magnifying glass to help users read the small type.

The longest entry in *The Oxford English Dictionary* is the verb 'set', which has over 430 senses consisting of approximately 60,000 words.

The term 'wooden spoon' – used for those who come last in an event – originated at Cambridge University during the early 19th century. The Maths student who got the lowest mark in the exam, yet still gained a third-class degree, was given an actual wooden spoon. This practice continued until 1909, when the system was changed so that the results were announced in alphabetical order rather than by exam mark, making it impossible to see who had come bottom.

The most frequently quoted work in *The Oxford English Dictionary*, with around 25,000 quotes, is the Bible.

It would take the average person sixty years to proof-read the whole of *The Oxford English Dictionary*.

'Underground' is the only word in the English language that begins and ends with the letters 'und'.

If someone in Northern Ireland said you had a 'ferntickle', they would be referring to a freckle.

The only fifteen-letter word that can be spelt without repeating a letter is 'uncopyrightable'.

The word 'tabloid' was invented by medical benefactor Sir Henry Wellcome. It refers to the paper size and not the style or content.

The most popular pet names used in Britain are Love, Mate, Duck, Babe, Sweetheart, Honey, Pet, Chuck, Darling and Lover.

A 2009 study found that 87% of Britons swear on a daily basis, with the average person uttering fourteen expletives every day.

No word in the English language rhymes with 'month', 'orange', 'silver' and 'purple'.

The words 'bookkeeper' and 'bookkeeping' are said to be the only ones in the English language with three consecutive double letters.

'The', 'of', 'and', 'a' and 'in' are the most common written words in the English language, while 'be', 'the', 'I', 'you' and 'and' are the most common spoken words.

The use of 'furlong' as a unit of distance comes from the Old English word 'fuhrling', meaning the length of a furrow. The distance, an eighth of a mile (1.3 km), was said by farmers to be the ideal length for a field, as it was the distance a herd of oxen could plough before needing a rest.

'Rhinotillexomania' is the medical term for nose picking.

The letters K, Q, V and Z do not appear in the Welsh alphabet.

There are two words in the English language that have all five vowels in order: 'abstemious' and 'facetious'.

GREAT BRITISH ANIMALS AND WILDLIFE

A survey by the PDSA, the UK's foremost veterinary charity, found the ten most popular names for a cat in Britain are: Tigger, Sooty, Felix, Lucky, Smokey, Charlie, Fluffy, Molly, Tiger and Smudge.

The ten most popular names for a dog are: Max, Ben, Buster, Tyson, Lady, Jack, Sam, Charlie, Molly and Tara…

… while for rabbits, the most popular name is Thumper, followed by Fluffy, Snowy and Rabbit.

During World War II, the British Air Ministry ordered the destruction of peregrine falcons due to the threat they posed to carrier pigeons.

Great spotted woodpeckers make their distinctive knocking sound by hitting the wood of a tree with their bills forty times a second.

Not all spiders spin webs.

The modern circus was founded by Philip Astley in 1768. He was an English trick-rider who found that centrifugal force made it easy to stand on a horse's back while it galloped round in a circle.

Pongo, the canine hero of *The Hundred and One Dalmatians*, was named after author Dodie Smith's own pet Dalmatian. Smith got the idea for her novel when she was walking two of her spotted dogs along the street, and passed a woman who loudly remarked: 'Those dogs would make a lovely fur coat!'

A 2008 study by the University of Portsmouth revealed that greenhouse gases produced by cow burps are growing at a faster rate than the man-made emissions responsible for global warming. Experts found that a herd of 200 cows can produce annual emissions of methane roughly equivalent to driving a family car more than 100,000 miles (160,000 km) on more than 4,707 gallons (21,400 litres) of petrol.

Ostriches are designated as dangerous animals in the UK and licences are needed to keep them. They are capable of killing you with a kick.

In 2008, scientists from the University of London's Birkbeck College found that 72% of dogs placed in a room with a yawning man would also yawn. The report suggested this was not out of tiredness or boredom, but as a way of empathising with their master.

When baby millipedes emerge from their eggs, they have short bodies and only three pairs of legs. They have to moult several times to allow both their bodies and their many pairs of legs to grow.

Holly the mongrel dog evaded capture in Cornwall for four years, after escaping from a kennel. She avoided traps, nets and bait laced with tranquilisers before finally walking into a house in Liskeard. The residents recognised her from pictures in the press and shut her in.

According to a 2009 survey by an equine social networking site, nine out of ten female riders would rather spend more time with their horses than with their partners.

The highest-flying British bird is the whooper swan. A pilot recorded a flock flying at just over 21,000 ft (8,230 m) over the Hebrides.

The very first bomb dropped by the Allies on Berlin during World War II killed the only elephant in the Berlin Zoo.

A fly can beat its wings in just 0.001 seconds.

A leech farm in Wales sells 15,000 leeches a year to the NHS. They are said to be particularly useful in plastic surgery, such as breast reconstruction and where a part of the body has become severed and has had to be sewn back on.

According to a team at Newcastle University's School of Agriculture, the happier a cow is, the more milk it produces. The study found that if cattle were treated with more kindness and consideration, their milk production could increase by up to 500 pints (284 litres) a year.

Although the dog show Crufts was founded in 1891, it has only been organised by The Kennel Club since 1942, after it bought the rights from the widow of Charles Cruft, a dog-food salesman.

Contrary to the song made popular by Vera Lynn, bluebirds have never flown over the 'White Cliffs of Dover' – they are natives of America.

A 2004 Oxford University Research project found there were 20,000 wild parrots, including parakeets, living in England, with the largest concentration around London and the south-east.

A blue tit weighs the same as a pound coin.

At the end of the snowdrop's pointy leaf is a toughened shield, which enables it to push through frozen earth.

Queen Victoria is reputed to have smoked cigarettes on her visits to Scotland in an attempt to deter midges.

A cow produces 140 times more saliva in a day than a human does.

Some dinosaurs were named before the word 'dinosaur' was invented. 'Dinosauria' meaning 'terrible lizards', was not proposed until 1842 by British anatomist Richard Owen.

Two dogs survived the sinking of the *Titanic*. They escaped on early lifeboats carrying so few people that no one objected. Margaret Hays brought her Pomeranian with her in lifeboat Number 7, while Henry Sleeper Harper boarded boat Number 3 with his Pekinese, Sun Yat Sen.

It is not true that one dog year equals seven human years. It actually depends on the size and weight of the dog and life stage they are at. For instance, a Jack Russell of age thirteen would be about sixty-six in human years, but a Saint Bernard would be nearer eighty-three.

During the first four days of World War II, 400,000 Londoners had their cats and dogs destroyed, for fear of their pets being terrified by the bombs or starving during the war.

There are about fifty species of ants in the UK. They will usually live for between forty-five and sixty days.

The stag beetle is the biggest beetle in Britain and can be up to 3.3 in (85 mm) long.

There are more than 6 million dogs in the UK. They produce 886 tons (900 tonnes) of faeces a day.

The sea eagle is the UK's largest bird of prey, and the fourth largest eagle in the world.

Sharks have no bones in their body. Their skeletons are made of cartilage.

A mole will die of starvation if it does not eat every few hours.

The blackbird is usually the first bird to start singing during the dawn chorus, which actually starts before sunrise. It is followed in turn by the song thrush, robin, wren, great tit and chaffinch before all the others join in.

In 2008, the world's first canine theatre production took place at an arts festival in Glasgow. The show *Who Stole my Sausage?* featured sights, sounds and smells designed to capture the attention of the four-legged audience.

Items that appear in London Zoo's yearly shopping list include: 46 tons (47 tonnes) of hay, 27.5 tons (28 tonnes) of straw, 0.5 tons (0.5 tonnes) of sultanas, 38,000 eggs, 28.5 tons (29 tonnes) of bananas, 29 tonnes of apples, 15,860 lettuces and 1,716 pints (975 litres) of milk.

The Labrador Retriever has been the most popular breed of dog in Britain since 1989.

A single edition of a daily newspaper uses the wood from approximately 5,000 trees to make the paper.

Bats produce the largest babies in the animal kingdom. An 0.3-oz (8-g) mother pipistrelle bat may produce a 0.07-oz (2-g) baby, which is 25% of its body weight. They can only produce one baby a year.

A cat who became trapped behind a bathroom cabinet survived for 44 days by licking condensation off the pipes.

During the 17th century, King George I decreed all pigeon droppings to be the property of the Crown, as pigeon manure was used in the making of gunpowder. Pigeon lofts were policed to enforce the law.

A queen bee has to eat eighty times her own weight to produce 2,000 eggs per day. Meanwhile, the average worker bee will fly approximately 500 miles (805 km) before it wears out and dies.

According to the 2009 Big Garden Birdwatch, run by the Royal Society for the Protection of Birds, the most common bird seen in gardens across Britain is the sparrow, followed by the starling, blackbird, blue tit, chaffinch, woodpigeon, collared dove, great tit, robin and long-tailed tit.

The long-tailed tit used to be known in Britain as the bumbarrel.

The average tree will drink around 3,520 pints (2,000 litres) of water each year.

Worms can have more than one heart, with some having five or ten.

Worms can also eat their own weight in food in a day.

Eighty different species of fish can be found in the River Thames.

In England in the 18th century, tax exemption was granted to drover dogs, which helped drive the herds to market. To mark these dogs, their tails were docked.

More than 500 British churchyards contain yew trees, with many of them older than the churches themselves.

Ducks' feet contain no nerves or blood vessels, which means they can swim in freezing water. Their webbed feet act like paddles for the ducks, but also mean that they can't walk and have to waddle instead.

Although black rats are now one of the rarest mammals in the UK, having largely been replaced by the brown rat, they can still be found around port towns, such as Liverpool, London, the Shiant Islands and Lundy island.

Brown rats first came to Britain during the 18th century thanks to the shipping trade from foreign countries.

The largest badger set ever found contained 130 entrances, fifty rooms, and 0.5 miles (0.8 km) of tunnels.

Fifty thousand badgers and 15,000 hedgehogs are killed on British roads every year.

The British bulldog was originally bred to be used in bull baiting during the 16th and 17th centuries. The practice was finally banned in 1835.

Bird faeces is white because of chemical reactions that occur within the urinary system to process waste matter into a substance that can be safely excreted with the least water loss. It is not actually the faeces that is white but the uric acid, which is the bird equivalent of human urine.

A bedbug can live for six months.

Only the female wasp stings.

The average worker bee makes only half a teaspoon of honey in its entire lifetime.

A dog's sense of smell is thirty times better than that of a human.

A cat from the West Midlands was nicknamed 'Macavity' (after the clever feline in T.S. Eliot's *Old Possum's Book of Practical Cats*) when in 2007 it started using the Number 331 bus several times a week. It would get onto the Walsall to Wolverhampton bus at the same stop most mornings, before jumping off at the next stop down the road, which was near a fish and chip shop.

In 2006, Flook the Burmese cat received a telegram from the Queen upon reaching her 100th birthday. It was actually 100 cat years – around twenty-three human years.

The ladybird is a member of the beetle family.

When Nora Hardwell died the day before her ninetieth birthday, she ensured her two collies, Tina and Kate, would live out the rest of their days in comfort. In her will, she left them the run of her home along with 5 acres (2 hectares) of land in Peasedown St John, near Bath, as well as £450,000 to be spent on their every whim. The will also stipulated that a carer must be employed to look after the two dogs, and that the house must be kept clean at all times.

The bird depicted on the logo of the RSPB is the avocet. It colonised Britain when coastal marshes in East Anglia were flooded to provide a defence against possible invasion by the Germans.

During World War II, a collie called Rob, who was a working farm dog, played a vital role in the war effort after being parachuted in behind enemy lines with his SAS unit. He was trained to watch over and protect the exhausted men as they slept in between carrying out their undercover operations. He made over twenty descents during his time with units in north Africa and Italy.

A sparrow has around 3,000 feathers during the summer and 3,500 in winter.

Commando the racing pigeon worked hard for the British forces during World War II, carrying out ninety trips in German-occupied France. He brought back messages to the UK in metal canisters strapped to its legs. He was awarded the Dickin Medal for animal bravery in 1945, the animal equivalent of the Victoria Cross.

A more recent recipient of the award was Buster, a Springer Spaniel, who played a vital role alongside the troops serving in Iraq. In March 2003, the unit he was with was conducting a dawn raid on some premises where caches of arms and explosives were thought to be held by extremists. When a thorough search by the men revealed nothing, Buster was sent in. Within minutes he had located the well-hidden arms that would have been used to devastating effect against the armed forces.

Other animals to be heralded for bravery in wartime include horses, dolphins, elephants and glow-worms.

Adders are Britain's only venomous snakes. They are so secretive and non-aggressive, however, that they are not regarded as a real threat to humans.

A single hedgehog can eat 250 slugs in one night.

The average hedgehog is covered in 5,000–7,000 spines, although there is none on the face, chest or legs.

Wild boar and brown bears both used to roam the UK before becoming extinct, boars in the 17th century and bears in the 11th century.

Every year, the RSPCA is called out to deal with approximately 1,500 road accidents involving deer.

After beating a thousand opponents in a 500-mile (805-km) race, Percy the racing pigeon finally landed in his Sheffield loft – only to be eaten by a cat.

Basking sharks, which are most commonly seen off the west coast of the UK, are among the biggest mammals in the world. Most sharks are around 98 ft (30 m) in length and are similar in size and weight to a double-decker bus. They are called basking sharks because many years ago fishermen saw them close to the surface and thought they were sun bathing.

Dragonflies are the fastest insects in the UK. The can travel at speeds of up to 30 mph (48 km/h).

The fastest bird in the UK is the peregrine falcon, which can swoop at up to 60 mph (96.6 km/h).

Male houseflies live for around seventeen days, while the female lives for around twenty-nine days.

During the 18th century, when Old English Sheepdogs actually worked as sheepdogs, no one groomed the dogs and they were sheared annually along with the sheep. The farmers' wives spun the dog shearings as well as the sheep's wool into warm clothing.

The third most popular pet behind a cat and a dog is a rabbit, with 1.6 million owners in the UK.

Biologists at Plymouth University found that fish could be trained to push levers at certain times of day to dispense food, making them rather smarter than most people believe.

A yew tree in Fortingall churchyard, north of Loch Tay, is over 5,000 years old, and is believed to be the oldest tree in Europe. During the last few hundred years however, as its fame has grown, souvenir hunters have begun to take large sections of the tree, so a wall had to be built round it to protect it. Some of its branches only survive because they are propped up.

The numbers of robins in Britain have increased by 20% in the past 25 years...

... however, the bullfinch population in Britain has declined by 62% in the last 35 years.

There are 56 native species of butterfly currently resident in Great Britain.

Only a few adult butterflies are capable of surviving the Great British winter, as they are unable to endure our cold temperatures.

The term 'warren', which is now used to describe rabbit colonies and burrows, actually comes from the name that was given to the walled enclosures that were built by Britons hundreds of years ago to keep their rabbits in.

The longest-ever jump by a dog was by a greyhound named Bang. He jumped 30 ft (9.1 m) while chasing a hare at Brecon Lodge, Gloucestershire, England, in 1849. He cleared a 4-ft 6-in-tall (1.4-m) gate and landed on a hard road, damaging his pastern bone.

The National Botanic Garden of Wales in the Vale of Tywi near Carmarthen has the world's largest single-span glasshouse, measuring 213 ft (65 m) long by 180 ft (55 m) wide.

The Natural History Museum in London holds over 27 million specimens in its collection.

The oldest bird ever recorded in Britain was a Manx shearwater that was ringed in 2004. It was an incredible 52 years old.

By the 1960s, 80% of the British peregrine falcon population had died due to pesticide poisoning.

While Dolly the sheep became the first mammal to be cloned from adult cells in 1996, the very first cloned mammals were Welsh Mountain ewes Morag and her twin sister Megan, who were cloned from embryo cells a year earlier in 1995 by researchers at the Roslin Institute in Scotland.

Dolly's name was inspired by the fact that the cell used to create her came from a mammary gland, so she was named after buxom country and western singer Dolly Parton.

Britons own more than 49 million pets, with just over 6 million households owning at least one cat, 5.2 million possessing at least one dog and just over 2 million households possessing goldfish.

Seventy-five per cent of British wrens were thought to have died during the harsh winter of 1962–63. However they recovered to become the most abundant birds in the UK.

The tallest tree in Britain is to be found in Dunkeld, Perthshire, where a Douglas Fir stands at a height of 213 ft (65 m).

Canada geese were first introduced to the UK in 1665, as an addition to the waterfowl collection of King Charles II at St James's Park.

vThere are 850 seaside donkeys still working in this country.

In 2008, a law was passed stating that children weighing more than 8 st (102 kg) are to be barred from riding on donkeys. The code also stated that donkeys could work only six days a week and must have a full day's rest. They must also have a rest of at least one hour at lunchtime or in the early evening.

Donkeys were first brought to Britain to work down mines. They can live to the age of fifty.

Grey squirrels were only introduced to the UK from the USA in the late 19th and early 20th century. Their success has been to the detriment of our native red squirrels.

In 2007, Goldie, a 15-year-old goldfish from Kent, was named the largest goldfish in Britain, after being measured at 1 ft 3 inches (42.7 cm) long, 5 inches (12.7 cm) high and weighing in at 2 lb (0.9 kg).

There are at least 1,500 different species of wildflower in the UK.

39 per cent of pet owners say they have more pictures of their pets than of their spouses.

The smallest dog on record belonged to Arthur Maples in the mid-1940s. The matchbox-sized Yorkshire terrier stood only 2.5 inches (6.4 cm) tall at the shoulder and measured only 3.5 inches (8.9 cm) from nose to tail. It weighed 4 oz (113 g) and died before its second birthday.

The number of barn owls has declined in Britain, due in part to the reduction of derelict old buildings and barns, many of which have been converted.

The UK has more than twenty types of toxic fungi that can kill humans.

During the 1950s, the rabbit population in the UK was so large that the Myxoma virus was deliberately introduced, killing 99% of all rabbits within just two years.

Slugs eat 35,000 tonnes) of potatoes every year in Britain.

There are thought to be around 44,000 beekeepers in the UK, who maintain around 274,000 colonies of honey bees.

Around the coasts of Great Britain there are seven species of starfish. Starfish may have as few as five arms, or as many as thirteen, depending on the species.

During the 1980s, the swans on the River Wensum baffled experts by all turning bright blue. The colour change turned out to be related to a nutritional deficiency, as the swans were living entirely off bread thrown in by passers-by and not eating a balanced diet. They went blue as a result.

Rats have sex up to twenty times a day.

Badgers can dig faster than a man with a spade.

Half of the world's population of grey seals are found on and around British coasts, and numbers here have doubled since 1960. Grey seals are protected by the Conservation of Seals Act, but individual seals causing damage to fishing nests can legally be killed.

Seven out of ten British dogs receive Christmas presents from their owners.

With a wingspan of 6–8 ft (1.8–2.4 m), the mute swan is Britain's largest bird.

Eighty-four per cent of all animal testing is done on rodents, with 12% on fish, amphibians and reptiles, 2.1% on large mammals, 1.4% on small mammals, 0.3% on cats and dogs and 0.1% on primates. Great apes such as chimpanzees are not allowed to be used in experiments.

The Goldcrest is the smallest bird in Britain, with a wingspan of just 5–6 inches (12.7–15.2 cm). It has to eat its own weight in food each day to survive the cold winter nights.

Almost half of all dogs and cats in the UK are overweight, although 76% of owners think their pet is a healthy weight.

One in four UK dog owners admits to never exercising themselves or their dogs. A study found the fattest dogs in the UK came from Nottingham.

Brown rats in the UK increased in size by 34% between 1998 and 2003, largely as the result of over-eating discarded fast food.

There are an estimated 77 million rats in the UK, with just over 75 million mice.

The brown hare is the fastest land mammal in the UK, able to reach speeds of up to 45 mph (72.4 km/h).

Robins do not migrate from the UK, but in winter robins from colder countries often migrate here. They have paler breasts and are less tame.

Many of the butterflies seen in Britain during the summer months have made their journey from Europe or Africa.

Primroses and polyanthus are the most common pot plants grown in this country.

The economic value of crops grown commercially in the UK that benefit from bee pollination is estimated at between £120 million and £200 million per annum.

Dozens of different blue tits can pass through a UK garden on a single day, even though there are never more than three or four at any one time.

Pest controller Steve North discovered a crocodile living in Peckham, south London, in 2008, while making a routine call about the council's pest control services. The 2-ft-long (61-cm) reptile was found in a bath in a flat. The resident had asked North to help him with a 'problem in his bathroom'.

The king cobra is the longest venomous snake in the world. The longest specimen ever recorded was kept at the London Zoo and measured an incredible 18 ft 9 inches (5.5 m). Zookeepers killed it in 1939 after the outbreak of war. They feared it would escape the zoo and pose a threat to the citizens of London.

The largest bird nest ever found in Britain belonged to a pair of golden eagles and measured more than 15 ft (4.6 m) deep.

Ranidaphobia is a fear of frogs.

There are sixteen species of bat in Britain and all are protected under the Wildlife and Countryside Act.

Three-quarters of all donkeys in Britain live in donkey sanctuaries.

In the 12th century in Britain, only noble-born people were allowed to hunt rabbits for food. The punishment for poaching was severe and could mean transportation for the offenders. In the late 19th century, the rabbit population reached large numbers and the Ground Game Act was passed by which tenants living off the land were allowed to hunt rabbits.

Female salmon die only a few days after laying their eggs.

In London there are said to be as many as twenty-eight foxes per square mile (or nearly eleven per square km).

GREAT BRITISH CRIME AND PUNISHMENT

In 1831, a boy of nine was hanged for arson.

Until 1879, British soldiers convicted of bad conduct were tattooed with the initials 'BC' (bad character), while deserters were marked with the letter 'D 'to prevent them from re-enlisting.

The trial of four people charged with running a London brothel was halted after an allegation that one of the jurors was a client.

The last public hanging took place on 26 May 1868, when Michael Barrett was executed outside Newgate prison, London, for his part in the Fenian bomb that killed twelve people outside Clerkenwell prison the previous year. Public hanging was abolished three days later, after which time all hangings took place within prison walls.

14, 000 police constables from every force in Britain were used during the G8 conference at Gleneagles in Scotland in July 2005.

During the early 19th century, William Burke and William Hare moved to Scotland from Ulster to work as labourers on the Union Canal. Ever aware of a market to meet, Burke and Hare set themselves up as procurers of human bodies to satisfy the demand of Edinburgh's medical schools. Originally the two would dig up the graves of the recently departed in the dead of night, but later started murdering people in Edinburgh's old town. They killed at least 16 people before being arrested in 1828. Hare gave evidence against Burke, who was hanged, while Robert Knox – the doctor who bought most of Burke and Hare's bodies without question – was never prosecuted.

Before women were commonly employed as full police officers, many police forces employed uniformed women with limited powers to search and look after female prisoners and deal with matters specifically affecting women and children. These female officers were often known as 'police matrons'.

Leicestershire baker Colin Pitchfork, who killed two schoolgirls in 1983 and 1986, was the first British criminal to be arrested and charged using DNA fingerprinting.

Policemen who arrested a burglar on the roof of a bank in Kent had to be rescued by fire officers after they became stuck.

Britain's worst female serial killer is said to be Mary Ann Cotton, who is believed to have killed at least twenty people over a twenty-year time period. She was eventually caught when a post-mortem examination on one of her children revealed arsenic poisoning as the cause of death. She was convicted of six murders in 1873 and hanged in Durham jail.

Magistrates in Cornwall abandoned a motoring case when the policeman due to give evidence said he had to go home to baby-sit.

The City of Glasgow Police is the oldest force in the world, twenty-nine years older than the Metropolitan Police formed under Sir Robert Peel.

Westminster Council revealed in December 2008 that foreign embassies in central London owed more than £1.5 million in unpaid parking fines, including one Sudanese diplomat who owed £37,000 for 349 separate tickets.

Dr Crippen, the infamous wife-murderer, was the first criminal to be caught thanks to radio. He and his mistress left London in July 1910 aboard a Canadian liner. The captain was suspicious of the couple and wired a description to his company, who promptly informed Scotland Yard. Officers were dispatched aboard a faster ship, and arrested Crippen when the ship docked.

John Haigh, who was hanged for murder in Wandsworth prison in London in 1949, used a drum of sulphuric acid to dissolve his victims' bodies. He was convicted of murdering widow Olive Durand-Deacon, however, after her dentures and gallstones survived the acid bath.

More than 35,000 people apply to join the police each year, yet only 5,000 are successful.

White cars are the most likely to be stolen. The RAC say this is because white paint is non-metallic and is easier to disguise through re-spraying.

The first police car chase in Britain took place through the streets of Northampton in 1899. The criminal was finally caught and arrested by Sergeant Hector McLeod.

Britain's longest-serving prisoner died in jail in 2007, 55 years after he was convicted of murdering a five-year-old. John Straffen, from Bath, was 22 when he was found guilty in July 1952 of murdering schoolgirl Linda Bowyer. Straffen, who was seventy-seven when he died, was sentenced to death, although that was later reduced to life imprisonment.

Peter Anthony Allen and John Robson Welby were the last men to be hanged in the UK, on 13 August 1964, after being found guilty of stabbing a man during a robbery.

In 1886, Dr Henry Faulds, who had written a paper on fingerprinting, suggested the concept to the Metropolitan Police in London. The idea was dismissed. It was another fifteen years before the first United Kingdom Fingerprint Bureau was founded in Scotland Yard by Commissioner Edward Henry, who had experience of the technique from his time in India. On 27 June 1902, the first conviction by fingerprint evidence was obtained. Harry Jackson was given seven years' penal servitude for burglary, while in 1905 the Stratton murders saw the first convictions for murder on fingerprint evidence.

In Britain, half of all appeals against parking tickets are successful, yet drivers appeal against only 1% of tickets.

A 2008 survey by an insurance company named Nottingham as the riskiest place in the UK for household burglaries, followed by London, Bristol, Stockport and Leeds.

In 2008, a priest dialled 999 to complain that he was not allowed to use a toilet in a W.H. Smith store, while another man rang to report that shop staff had put unwanted mushrooms on his pizza. In a third incident, one caller dialled 999 to report Santa was breaking into a house with Rudolf.

The first motor vehicle owned by the Metropolitan Police had the registration number A209.

A man inadvertently foiled an attempted bank robbery after assuming it was an April Fool prank. Customer Andrew Stewart was reading a newspaper in his local bank on 31 March 2008 when a raider burst in claiming to be holding a gun inside his backpack, and demanded money. While terrified cashiers prepared to hand over a bundle of notes, Mr Stewart calmly walked up to the robber and said: 'It's April the 1st isn't it, mate? It's April Fool's Day' and took what was, in fact, an empty bag from him.

Antique-shop owner Edwin Bush was arrested in 1961 after police used the first Identikit picture to track him. Bush stabbed Elsie May Batten to death in Charing Cross Road, London, using an antique dagger. Within four days of the picture being issued, PC John Cole recognised Bush and arrested him on his beat in the Soho area of London.

Arthur Ferguson was a Scottish con artist who sold British national monuments and other government property to visiting American tourists during the 1920s. Among the national landmarks he 'sold' were: Nelson's Column in Trafalgar Square, for which he received £6,000; Big Ben, for which he took £1,000 as a down payment; and Buckingham Palace, another £2,000 for a down payment.

The first thousand members of Robert Peel's police dressed in blue tailcoats and top hats. The uniform was carefully selected to make them look more like ordinary citizens, rather than soldiers.

According to the latest British Crime Survey, more than half of all offences involve gain or attempted gain, such as burglaries, theft and attempted theft.

Two members of Robert Peel's London Police Force were killed during its first year in operation between 1829 and 1830. Very unpopular, they were often pelted with bricks and bottles by the poor.

In 2009, a gang was branded Britain's worst burglars after drilling their way into an empty office next door to a bank. The thieves had hoped to break into the Royal Bank of Scotland branch in Poynton, near Macclesfield, Cheshire, but having forced their way into the wrong property, they tried and failed again to get into the bank and left empty-handed.

In England, if a condemned man survived three attempts to hang him, his sentence would automatically be commuted to life imprisonment.

Britain's biggest-ever robbery took place on 22 February 2006, at the Securitas depot in Tonbridge, Kent. The family of the depot manager were kidnapped and the robbers got away with more than £53 million.

GREAT BRITISH
TELEVISION

In 1971, sales of hairdryers dropped dramatically in Britain after *Coronation Street* character Val Barlow was electrocuted by hers.

Only thirteen episodes of the children's TV classics *Mr Benn* and *Bagpuss* were ever made.

Inspector Morse creator Colin Dexter appeared as an extra in every episode of the programme.

At the age of nineteen, chat-show legend Sir Michael Parkinson was one of Britain's youngest-ever army captains and served during the Suez Operation.

Doctor Who baddies the Cybermen were originally created to fill the void left by the Daleks, when their creator Terry Nation went off to make films with them and tried to set them up with their own series in America.

The ten actors that have played the Doctor on television are William Hartnell, Patrick Troughton, Jon Pertwee, Tom Baker, Peter Davison, Colin Baker, Sylvester McCoy, Paul McGann, Christopher Ecclestone and David Tennant. Matt Smith becomes the eleventh Doctor in 2010.

J.K. Rowling was once asked to write an episode of *Doctor Who* but she declined.

The famous Andrex puppy commercials were first screened in 1972. The original concept included a little girl running through her house trailing a roll of Andrex. However, this was blocked by television regulators who believed it would encourage children to be wasteful. So, the little girl was replaced by a playful Labrador puppy.

Cheryl Cole was the first member of Girls Aloud to be voted into the band on reality show *Popstars: The Rivals*.

The actress Peggy O'Neil was the first person ever to be interviewed on television, at the ideal Home Exhibition in Southampton in 1930.

In February 2005, the then PM Tony Blair helped viewer Vivien Colville win £6,000 on *Richard and Judy's* competition 'You Say We Pay' when he played the game in Richard's place.

Catherine Tate, Russell Brand, Paul O'Grady, David Tennant and Keira Knightly have all appeared in *The Bill*.

Meanwhile, Kate Winslet, Minnie Driver and *Pirates of the Caribbean* actor Orlando Bloom all had parts in the long-running medical drama *Casualty* before making it big in Hollywood.

Midsomer Murders is shown in 206 territories across the world, including the United States.

Midsomer Murders star John Nettles once knocked on a door during filming and announced himself as Detective Sergeant Bergerac.

Leslie Grantham originally auditioned for the part of Pete Beale in *EastEnders*. The BBC, however, decided he was too handsome to play a fruit-and-vegetable stall trader and offered him the part of 'Dirty' Den Watts.

In December 2008, a woman dialled 999 furious she could not get through to vote for *Strictly Come Dancing* winner Tom Chambers.

The original *Come Dancing* programme, which began in 1949, was created by Miss World supremo Eric Morley to teach the public about the joy of dancing. It wasn't until 1953 that the show concentrated on the competition element, with couples from all over the UK competing for the coveted *Come Dancing* trophy.

Cigarette advertising on television was banned on 31 July 1965, although adverts for pipe tobacco and cigars, which were seen as being much safer, were allowed to continue for another quarter of a century.

Little Britain started life as a radio programme on BBC Radio 4.

Theatre critic Kenneth Tynan became the first person to use the 'f-word' on British television on 13 November 1965. It led to outrage across the country and even in the House of Commons, where Prime Minister Harold Wilson was obliged to pass comment.

Not all viewers could see Channel 4 when it launched in November 1982; it took five years for all transmitters in England, Scotland and Northern Ireland to be adapted. However, the network will only become fully available in Wales when its switch to digital TV is complete in 2010, twenty-eight years after it went on air.

Only Fools and Horses star Nicholas Lyndhurst was the initial choice to play detective Jonathan Creek. The role eventually went to Alan Davies.

Hans Zimmer, the composer who has won Oscars, Grammies and Golden Globes for his soundtracks for the likes of *The Lion King, Gladiator, Driving Miss Daisy,* and *The Da Vinci Code*, also composed the theme tune to *Going for Gold*.

Newsnight's Jeremy Paxman became the focus of media attention himself in 2000 when the stolen Enigma machine that had been taken from Bletchley Park Museum was inexplicably sent to him in the post. He returned it.

Clangers and *Bagpuss* creator Peter Firmin brought Basil Brush to life in 1963. He was paid £12 to make him, receiving just £1 for each of the puppet's appearances.

The longest-running programme on British television is *Panorama*, which was first broadcast on 11 November 1953. The programme's first editor, Dennis Bardens, came up with the programme name as he looked out at the panoramic view from his office, which he described as 'very capacious'.

In 2009, a portrait of Colin Firth as *Pride and Prejudice*'s Mr Darcy sold at auction for £12,000. The picture was a prop that had hung in the dashing character's country house in the 1995 BBC adaptation of the Jane Austen's classic novel.

Adrian Chiles was the most-watched television presenter in 2008, with a combined audience of over 1 billion, having hosted not only *The One Show,* but also *Match of the Day 2* and *The Apprentice – You're Fired*, as well as featuring in coverage of the 2008 Beijing Olympics.

Anne Robinson developed her trademark wink during her time as presenter of *Points of View*. The director told her not to wink, so she insisted on winking at the end of every programme from then on.

Only 20,000 people watched the first-ever edition of *Match of the Day*, which was shown on BBC2 in August 1964 and featured highlights of Liverpool v Arsenal. The figure was less than half that of the crowd at the match itself.

Lord Sebastian Coe was the first British athlete to be allowed to use his own name to promote products on television when he advertised Horlicks in 1982.

When Arthur Fowler was sent to prison in *EastEnders*, a couple turned up at the set of the soap and offered to look after his allotment until he got out.

In 1995, there were 225 television programmes in Britain watched by more than 15 million people. In 2004, only ten programmes achieved that viewing figure.

Sir David Attenborough was initially discouraged from appearing on screen because his BBC boss thought his teeth were too big.

Attenborough has received hate mail from viewers for not crediting God in his nature programmes.

The cast of *Emmerdale* gets through forty-five pairs of Wellington boots every year.

Ten thousand miles of cabling runs through BBC Broadcasting House in London.

The pilot episode for *The Office* had a budget of just £90,000.

None of the filming for *The Office* took place in Slough, apart from the opening title sequence.

Coronation Street has more than 90,000 cobblestones on it.

When *Mastermind* began in 1972, it was broadcast late at night as it was considered to be too academic for a mainstream audience.

Arthur Lowe was originally asked to play the role of Sergeant Wilson in *Dad's Army*, with John Le Mesurier playing the part of Captain Mainwaring. They decided they each preferred the other's role.

Television legend Sir David Frost began his career as a reporter for a local television news programme. His bosses weren't impressed by his efforts, however, and believing that he didn't have a future in regional broadcasting, refused to renew his contract.

The highest-ever audience for a game show came on 22 December 1978, when 21.2 million people tuned into ITV's *Sale of the Century*. Industrial action had led to a complete halt in production at the BBC.

The longest-ever advert to be shown on British television was broadcast on Christmas Day 1977. It was for British Rail and lasted seven minutes.

The pilot of the sitcom *Yes, Minister* was made in 1977, but a full series of the show was not produced until after the 1979 general election, as there were fears that it might influence the public.

Last of the Summer Wine is the world's longest-running sitcom.

It was *Crackerjack*'s first presenter, Eamonn Andrews, who devised the legendary game Double or Drop, and when he left the show in 1964 he took the format with him. It was not until the 1970s that a deal was made with Andrews and the game returned.

The word 'crackerjack' dates from the 1800s and means 'a superb or wonderful thing'.

The pints pulled at the Rovers Return in *Coronation Street* are actually shandy.

Several *Countdown* viewers have asked to use the programme's theme tune at their funerals.

Bruce Forsyth is one of only two men known to have slept with two Miss Worlds. The other was George Best, who claimed to have slept with three.

In November 2008, Anthony Gormley's design model for his *Angel of the North* sculpture became the first £1 million object to be valued on BBC1's *Antiques Roadshow*.

Around 2,000 people turn up to an *Antiques Roadshow* recording. The experts usually view around 10,000 items, which have an average value of £50.

John Cleese and Connie Booth took six weeks to write each episode of *Fawlty Towers*. The norm for an episode of a sitcom is ten days.

The *Blue Peter* dog Petra died after appearing on just one programme. She was replaced by a lookalike for the rest of her life.

The original *Blue Peter* ship logo was designed by legendary television artist Tony Hart.

In 2008, the TV Licensing Authority issued around 35,000 licences for black-and-white TVs, down from 212,000 in 2000. The cost of a licence is £47, which compares very favourably with the £139.50 you have to pay for a colour TV licence.

X Factor supremo Simon Cowell was asked to be on the judging panel for the original *Popstars* series, which launched the career of Hear'say. He refused: not only did he believe that the show would not be popular with viewers, but he was also worried that it would reveal too much about what went on behind the scenes in the music industry.

Blockbusters host Bob Holness received letters of complaint from viewers who thought that his habit of stretching out his arm to welcome a new contestant was actually a Nazi salute.

The idea for *Newsround* came after a survey revealed that only 0.7% of children watched the news.

The 1977 *Morecambe and Wise Christmas Special* was watched by over 27 million people, which was more than half the UK population at that time.

My Family star Robert Lindsay was first choice to play the psychologist Cracker, but he turned down the role. It was given to Robbie Coltrane.

TV game show *Who Wants to be a Millionaire?* is insured by Lloyd's of London against having to pay major cash prizes.

Anna Ford and Reginald Bosanquet used to play darts in the production office before going on air to read the ITN News.

Ford was told she was too old to become a newsreader when she joined Granada television as a researcher, aged thirty, in 1974. She read her last news bulletin in 2006, aged sixty-two.

Play School was unexpectedly the first ever programme broadcast on BBC2 on 21 April 1964. A grand opening for the channel had been planned for the night before, but was blacked out by a power failure.

Simon Cowell won £20 of kitchen utensils on *Sale of the Century* in 1990.

AND A FEW FINAL BITS...

 Britain's longest-married couple are Frank and Anita Milford from Plymouth, who were wed on 26 May 1928. After the wedding ceremony, they went to see a Charlie Chaplin film.

 At school, Archbishop of Canterbury Dr Rowan Williams had a note permanently excusing him from sports.

 A record-breaking power surge of 3,000 megawatts hit the National Grid after people had finished watching the solar eclipse in 1999. The surge was enough to make 5 million cups of tea. The previous record was 2,800 megawatts, which happened in 1990 during England's football World Cup shoot-out with West Germany.

A study by the British Cheese Board found that eating different types of cheese can affect your dreams. Those who eat Stilton are more likely to have vivid dreams, while Red Leicester is said to bring on nostalgic dreams, with lovers of Cheshire cheese more likely to have a completely dreamless night.

In late 1952, some British film producers paid £5,000 for the film rights to Agatha Christie's *The Mousetrap*, which had just opened in the West End. The only proviso was that the film could not be made until six months after the play had closed. More than half a century later, it is still going strong and remains the longest-running play in history. The film producers did not last as long.

A recent survey found that British housewives spend almost half their free time using the Internet. This is not only a higher proportion that British students and the unemployed, but more than housewives in 15 other countries around the globe including Japan, China, Germany, and the United States, where women spend just 38 per cent of their leisure time surfing the web.

Many people believe that the reason why both the daffodil and the leek have become national emblems of Wales is that the word for both is the same in Welsh: 'cenhinen' – leek; 'cenhinen pedr' – daffodil. The result of this confusion is that both have been adopted as national emblems.

According to The British Association of Aesthetic Plastic Surgeons, the top ten surgical procedures for men and women in 2008 were: breast augmentation, blepharoplasty (eyelid surgery), face/neck lift, breast reduction, abdominoplasty (tummy tuck), liposuction, rhinoplasty (nose correction), otoplasty (ear correction) and brow lifts. Women accounted for 91% of procedures.

The British flag is officially called the 'Union Flag'. Technically, it should only be called the Union Jack when it is flown from the jack mast of a ship.

Lilies are the most popular flowers sent by Interflora.

The vocal coach who taught American actor Dick Van Dyke to speak in a memorably erratic Cockney accent for the film *Mary Poppins* actually came from Lancashire.

British women buy 98 million pairs of shoes each year.

Under a never-revoked rule, the head boy at Blundell's School in Tiverton, Devon, is permitted to keep a pig at school and a mistress in town.

Meanwhile, at Felsted School in Essex, the head boy or girl may still smoke a pipe, grow a beard or keep a goat.

Each year over 984 tons (1,000 tonnes) of fat cause 36,000 sewer blockages in Thames Water's region.

Over 9 million red roses are given in Britain every Valentine's Day.

The longest-ever title for a British film was *The Persecution and Assassination of Jean-Paul Marat as Performed by the Inmates of the Asylum of Charenton under the Direction of the Marquis de Sade* (1966). The average number of letters used in a film title is seventeen.

Only 6% of British people flush the toilet while still sitting on it, compared to 33% of Americans.